Performance Evaluation

An Essential Management Tool

Edited by
Christine S. Becker

PRACTICAL MANAGEMENT SERIES
Barbara H. Moore, Editor

Performance Evaluation
Capital Financing Strategies for Local Governments
Creative Personnel Practices
Current Issues in Leisure Services
The Entrepreneur in Local Government
Hazardous Materials, Hazardous Waste
Human Services on a Limited Budget
Long-Term Financial Planning
Managing New Technologies
Police Management Today
Practical Financial Management
Productivity Improvement Techniques
Risk Management Today
Shaping the Local Economy
Successful Negotiating in Local Government
Telecommunications for Local Government

The Practical Management Series is devoted to the
presentation of information and ideas from diverse
sources. The views expressed in this book are those of
the contributors and are not necessarily those of the
International City Management Association.

Library of Congress Cataloging-in-Publication Data

Performance evaluation.
    (Practical management series)
    Bibliography: p.
    1. Local officials and employees—Rating of. I. Becker,
Christine Schwarz, 1949-   . II. Series.
JS155.P47   1988   352′.005142   88-6806
ISBN 0-87326-079-1

Printed in the United States of America.

939291908988
54321

Foreword

Performance evaluations are notorious for the anxiety they create in an organization—not only for employees whose work is under discussion but also for supervisors who must conduct these periodic appraisals. Yet the process has great positive potential if managers and supervisors can learn to use it as an opportunity for strengthening individual performance, developing employee potential, and improving organizational effectiveness.

Performance Evaluation: An Essential Management Tool builds on the success of ICMA's training package on the same subject and provides additional information and ideas for managers and supervisors. It presents diverse perspectives on performance and its determinants, shows examples of systems that have proven effective, and offers guidance for managers and supervisors who must carry out the evaluation process.

This book is part of ICMA's Practical Management Series, which is devoted to serving local officials' needs for timely information on current issues and problems.

We are grateful to Christine S. Becker for organizing and compiling the volume and to the organizations and individuals who granted ICMA permission to reprint their material. Thanks also go to David S. Arnold, who helped plan the entire Practical Management Series.

William H. Hansell, Jr.
Executive Director
International City
   Management Association

Performance Evaluation:
An Essential Management Tool

The International City Management Association is the professional and educational organization for chief appointed management executives in local government. The purposes of ICMA are to enhance the quality of local government and to nurture and assist professional local government administrators in the United States and other countries. In furtherance of its mission, ICMA develops and disseminates new approaches to management through training programs, information services, and publications.

Managers, carrying a wide range of titles, serve cities, towns, counties, and councils of governments in all parts of the United States and Canada. These managers serve at the direction of elected councils and governing boards. ICMA serves these managers and local governments through many programs that aim at improving the manager's professional competence and strengthening the quality of all local governments.

The International City Management Association was founded in 1914; adopted its City Management Code of Ethics in 1924; and established its Institute for Training in Municipal Administration in 1934. The Institute, in turn, provided the basis for the Municipal Management Series, generally termed the "ICMA Green Books."

ICMA's interests and activities include public management education; standards of ethics for members; the *Municipal Year Book* and other data services; urban research; and newsletters, a monthly magazine, *Public Management*, and other publications. ICMA's efforts for the improvement of local government management—as represented by this book—are offered for all local governments and educational institutions.

About the
Editor

Christine S. Becker is special assistant to the director of the Washington, D.C., Department of Corrections. Previously she was the chief of human resource development in the D.C. Office of Personnel. Before joining the District government in 1984, she worked at the International City Management Association as director of the Office of Education Services and director of training. She holds a bachelor's degree from Boston College and a master's degree in public administration from the University of Southern California Washington Public Affairs Center. She has completed all course work and qualifying examinations for a doctorate in public administration from the University of Southern California.

About the Authors

Following are the affiliations of the contributors to *Performance Evaluation* at the time of writing (if an author is not listed here, an affiliation was not available):

Gordon Anderson, MBA programs director, Strathclyde Business School, England.

Lloyd S. Baird, professor, School of Management, Boston University.

Kathryn M. Bartol, professor of organizational behavior and management of human resources, College of Business and Management, University of Maryland, College Park, Maryland.

Richard W. Beatty, professor of industrial relations and human resources, Rutgers University, New Brunswick, New Jersey.

Melvin Blumberg, head, Division of Business Administration, Pennsylvania State University–Harrisburg, Middletown, Pennsylvania.

Dan G. Brown, classification supervisor, City and County of Denver's Career Service Authority, Denver, Colorado.

Shelley R. Burchett, compensation and employment specialist, Pioneer Hi-Bred International, Inc., an agricultural firm headquartered in Des Moines, Iowa.

Ronald W. Clement, associate professor, College of Business and Public Affairs, Murray State University, Murray, Kentucky.

Ted Cocheu, principal, HRD Consulting, Los Gatos, California.

Kenneth P. De Meuse, human resources consultant, Intergraph Corporation, Huntsville, Alabama (affiliation at time of publication).

A. Arthur Geis, senior associate, Organizational Dynamics, Inc., Burlington, Massachusetts.

Kathleen Guinn, senior consultant, Development Dimensions International, Pittsburgh, Pennsylvania.

Linda Hopper, director of training, International City Management Association, Washington, D.C.

David Hulme, training officer, Strathclyde Passenger Transport Executive, England.

Barbara K. Malinauskas, principal, Consult Associates, Murray, Kentucky.

David C. Martin, assistant professor of management of human resources and director, personnel and industrial relations program, Kogod College of Business Administration, The American University, Washington, D.C.

Douglas McGregor, professor of management, School of Industrial Management, Massachusetts Institute of Technology.

Charles D. Pringle, head, Department of Management, James Madison University, Harrisonburg, Virginia.

Craig Eric Schneier, managing principal and national director, human resources and organization effectiveness practice, Sibson & Company, Inc., Princeton, New Jersey (affiliation at time of publication).

O. Glenn Stahl, retired executive, U.S. Civil Service Commission.

George E. Stevens, College of Business Administration, University of Central Florida.

Neil A. Stroul, president, Management & Training Innovations, Inc., McLean, Virginia.

Dawn Marie Warfle, curriculum development specialist, International City Management Association, Washington, D.C.

Ed Young, lecturer, Manchester Business School, Manchester, England.

Contents

Introduction

————————————— Christine S. Becker

Performance evaluation is traditionally seen as a personnel function. For a literature search on the subject, the primary resources are *personnel* journals and textbooks. This book of readings is no exception. Nearly all of the articles reprinted here are drawn from personnel resources. Yet shrewd managers and wise personnel directors know that performance evaluation must be much more than a personnel system if it is to meet the needs of both the organization and the individuals in it. Performance evaluation must be seen as a crucial management tool designed to strengthen individual performance, develop employee potential, and improve organizational effectiveness.

Few public managers today will question the importance or potential power of a well-designed performance evaluation process. Many, however, will admit that their evaluation systems fall short of expectations. In 1957, Douglas McGregor presented his now famous "uneasy look at performance appraisal," which is reprinted in this volume. McGregor raised questions then about the reasonableness of annual critical assessments that attempt to judge employee worth. He argued for a future-oriented approach that emphasizes employee development and involves the employee in deciding what is important. Although few would disagree with McGregor, managers are still struggling with how to apply their best management intuition and common sense to the development of successful performance evaluation processes.

The fundamental dilemma about performance evaluation can perhaps be reduced to a conflict inherent in an organization's desire to create an objective system to deal with what is essentially a subjective process. The larger the organization, the more intense the desire to standardize the system. This drive for objective, standardized, across-the-board systems loses sight of the basic purpose of performance evaluation—to provide feedback on *individual* performance based on clearly defined goals or expectations that will lead to improved performance in the future. There are many valid reasons for this struggle to develop standardized, objective systems:

1. Fear of litigation. The more standardized the system, the more defensible it is in court.
2. Lack of time. The more standardized and objective the system, the easier it is to administer.
3. Fear of confrontation. The more personal the system, the higher is the risk of confrontation and disagreement about ratings and feedback.
4. Discomfort with the evaluator's role. It is difficult to give personal and focused feedback to an individual. A standardized system with a uniform rating scale eases the discomfort.
5. The need for equity. A standardized, objective system is seen as a more equitable system even if it fails to provide a fair assessment of individual performance.

This book does not resolve the fundamental dilemma about performance evaluation. Instead, it provides perspectives on the issues that produce the dilemma to help managers make informed choices about meeting the needs of individual employees and the organization.

Part 1: Perspectives on performance appraisal

Part I provides a context for the book. In the opening article, Charles D. Pringle and Melvin Blumberg address some fundamental issues about job performance that should be considered when a manager is deciding how to evaluate performance. They argue that performance is a function of three variables—capacity, willingness, and opportunity. Although many performance evaluation systems take into account capacity and willingness, the opportunity factor is often missing.

The articles by Douglas McGregor and by Neil A. Stroul provide a valuable management perspective on performance appraisal. McGregor suggests that managers involve subordinates in setting goals and appraising progress so that the focus is on analyzing *future performance* possibilities rather than criticizing *past behavior.* Stroul argues for a developmental approach to performance appraisal that emphasizes the manager's role as a developer of people. Stroul believes that the dilemmas about performance appraisal can best be resolved by changing people's mindsets rather than by revising evaluation forms.

"Performance Appraisal and the Law," by Shelley R. Burchett and Kenneth P. De Meuse, is included in this section to remind all managers why careful attention to appraisal systems is important. The authors provide a summary of laws and court rulings that can have an impact on performance evaluation systems. They make a subtle but convincing argument for focusing on the mechanics of the performance evaluation process.

Part 2: Approaches to performance evaluation

The next five articles focus on developing appraisal systems. O. Glenn Stahl provides an overview of the issues, questions, and problems that managers must consider when developing appraisal systems. The next two articles reconfirm the importance of linking a performance appraisal system to the overall management philosophy and culture of the organization. Alva F. Kindall and James Gatza provide a five-step appraisal program that will help foster initiative, encourage imagination, develop a sense of responsibility, and intensify efforts to meet organizational goals. Writing more than twenty years later, Craig Eric Schneier, Richard W. Beatty, and Lloyd S. Baird present a similar framework for developing a performance management system that fosters improved manager-employee relations.

The last two articles in this section provide case studies on how two organizations revised their performance evaluation systems. Gordon Anderson, Ed Young, and David Hulme describe a process that was used in a British transit authority to minimize paperwork and maximize productive interaction between managers and employees. Ted Cocheu describes how one organization overhauled its performance appraisal system. The overhaul began out of frustration with an inconsistently applied trait-rating system and concluded with an organizationwide commitment to performance planning.

Part 3: Managing employee performance

The articles in the third section will help managers integrate their performance appraisal systems into an ongoing performance management process. Kathleen Guinn presents a three-part model for expanding the effectiveness of annual performance appraisals into a year-round management process. Similarly, the articles "Managing Employee Performance" and "Creating a Performance Management System" present step-by-step guidance for making performance appraisal one part of a complete management system.

No book on performance evaluation would be complete without some discussion of rewards, particularly financial rewards. The concept of merit pay is complex, controversial, and potentially powerful when implemented successfully. The private sector has relied more heavily on performance-based pay systems than has the public sector, but support for financial reward systems continues to be mixed at best. A. Arthur Geis suggests that faulty performance evaluation systems contribute to the controversy, confusion, and frustration over merit pay. He argues, like many of the authors in this book, for a performance management system that provides on-going review and feedback for all employees. Once a performance management system is in place, managers can more effectively link performance results to pay increases or bonuses.

Part 4: Developing performance standards

Next the book addresses one of the most difficult aspects of performance planning and management—developing standards. Even with the most informal evaluation systems, managers need something against which to gauge individual performance. The two articles in Part 4 present step-by-step processes for establishing standards, goals, and targets. Dan G. Brown describes a broad training format used in Denver, Colorado, to help managers develop meaningful and realistic performance standards. The next article, "Establishing Performance Goals and Standards," is adapted from a comprehensive training program that teaches supervisors how to establish performance standards, communicate about those standards, and evaluate performance in a productive and constructive way, using the agreed-upon standards. Taken together, these articles send a clear message that managers and supervisors must participate in training programs in order to develop the skill that is needed to establish performance standards.

Part 5: Communicating performance results

Nearly all of the articles in this book, in one way or another, touch on the importance of communication. The articles in the final section zero in on two specific aspects of successful communication—the appraisal interview and the process of training raters to communicate fairly and effectively. The first two articles, by Ronald W. Clement and colleagues, provide guidance on carrying out the face-to-face aspect of performance evaluation.

The last two articles address the fact that, to a large extent, the success of any performance evaluation system depends on a manager's ability to make informed judgments about employee performance and then share those judgments in a way that motivates employees. David C. Martin states that mangers play three roles in the evaluation process—coach, leader, and judge. The successful rater (manager) understands the three roles clearly and knows how to carry them out effectively.

The combination of articles in this volume provides an integrated view of the need for performance appraisal systems, how to develop them, issues involved in incorporating them into existing organizations, and the importance of training managers to use them and to communicate skillfully during appraisal interviews. The book underscores the value of a sound performance appraisal system in enhancing individual employee and organizational effectiveness.

PART 1

Perspectives on Performance Appraisal

What Really Determines Job Performance?

Charles D. Pringle and Melvin Blumberg

There are more behavioral science theories relating to the determinants of job performance than to any other aspect of human behavior in organizations. Some theories claim that employees are motivated by a drive to fulfill various needs. Others claim that the way to improve performance is to give people enriched jobs with more autonomy, challenge, and responsibility. Still other theories claim that the key to increasing performance is a better incentive system that links pay, promotion, and recognition to high job performance. A final set of theories claim that people will increase their performance when supervisors provide clearly specified, task-related goals that are moderately difficult to attain.[1,2]

As a whole, these theories concentrate on the individual worker, the organization's incentive system, leadership, or the characteristics of the worker's job. In an attempt to determine which of these theories best predicts job performance, we took a hard look at the research evidence. The results were surprisingly clear. We found that all of the theories predict job performance, but none of them very well. Why not? The following example sheds light on this problem.

The overlooked influence: an example

Consider, for instance, the case of two new management trainees who are equally intelligent, energetic, and ambitious. Both have equal desires to become high job performers and to climb the career ladder as rapidly as possible. Both are hired by the same company.

Reprinted by permission, *SAM Advanced Management Journal*, Autumn, 1986, Society for Advancement of Management, Cincinnati, OH 45206

Trainee A is assigned to the firm's western region, and Trainee B is assigned to the eastern region.

Both trainees begin their employment with equal levels of ability and drive to succeed. Six years later, A is the assistant vice president of corporate marketing making $75,000, while B is the marketing director of a medium-sized district within the eastern region making $38,000. Clearly, A's performance, as measured by advancement, responsibility, and salary, is much higher than B's. This difference in performance cannot be explained simply by differences in motivational need states, goals, incentive systems, or job enrichment. Both A and B had similar needs; they were both able to set clear, reasonably attainable goals; they worked under similar incentive systems; and they both had jobs that were full of challenge, autonomy, and responsibility. Hence, the difference in their performance can only be adequately explained by reference to the differences in each person's environment.

Six years ago, A was assigned to a district where everyone worked hard and did well. It was headed by a dynamic, hard-driving manager who surrounded himself with the same kind of people. In A's first assignment, she found herself in a work group of high performers who spent what few coffee breaks they took discussing their jobs and suggesting ways to do them better. A's first boss encouraged her to become active in outside professional associations, and instructed her to attend developmental seminars. This manager also protected her from unnecessary activities that would not help her grow and develop. Her bosses, over the six years, delegated steadily increasing amounts of responsibility to her as she proved her capabilities and gave her enough budget to hire and develop first-rate subordinates and to operate a first-class marketing program.

B, on the other hand, was initially assigned to a district where he had to go slow, protecting his turf, and cover himself with a lot of paperwork. His first boss, who had been in the job for fifteen years, did not belong to any professional associations and felt that going to outside seminars was a waste of time and money. He encouraged B to join the district softball team, to get into the football pools, and to "relax and enjoy coffee with the guys" each morning and afternoon. His favorite expression was "What's your hurry? Don't kill the job." Although his boss dumped a lot of his work onto B, he did not give him either the authority or budget to do the job right. While A was learning rapidly and being promoted, B was still trying to get a handle on his first job assignment.

The difference in the six-year performance level of these two managers cannot be explained by differences in the two individuals, their job characteristics, or the organization's incentive system. The only major difference between the two managers is that A had an attractive, demanding environment in which to perform and B did not—and this made all the difference.

This example emphasizes that certain situational constraints beyond the employee's control play a far stronger role in influencing job performance than is generally acknowledged in theories of performance. We call these situational constraints that help or hinder managers' performance, *opportunity*. As we see it, opportunity is made up of all the things happening around a manager and his job that help or hinder him in doing the job and are also beyond his direct control.

Dimensions of job performance

Obviously, more than opportunity is required for high job performance. It takes only a quick look at the theories of performance to see that they talk about a lot of things that are known to influence work performance. Aside from situational constraints, these can be organized into two general categories. The first of these categories has to do with a person's *capacity* to perform, i.e., having the physical and mental capabilities to perform a task effectively. This category includes such things as ability, knowledge, skills, intelligence, age, state of health, educational level, endurance, stamina, and energy level. The second category has to do with a manager's *willingness* to perform. This category includes the psychological and emotional characteristics that influence the degree to which an individual is inclined to perform a task. Here, we include such things as motivation level, job satisfaction, personality, attitudes, values, task characteristics, need states, perceived role expectations, job involvement, anxiety, and self-image.

Our point is that all three categories—opportunity, capacity, and willingness—must be present for high job performance to occur. We can write this as an equation:

$$P = f(O,C,W).$$

This equation says that performance (P) is a function (f) of three interacting categories—opportunity (O), capacity (C), and willingness (W).

If any one of these categories is missing or has a low value, then performance will not occur or will occur at a very low level. For instance, one of the authors visited a coal mine and was surprised one day to learn that there had been no coal production. A major cave-in had occurred and even the most capable and willing miners could not produce any coal until it was cleared. Hence, opportunity was zero. Similarly, a novice miner who has not yet been trained to mine coal might have high willingness and might be given the opportunity to substitute for an experienced miner who is sick. The novice, however, will mine little coal because his or her capacity (i.e., ability

Figure 1. The determinants of job performance.

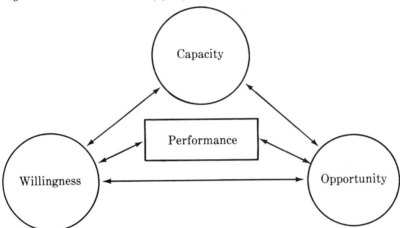

Source: Blumberg, Melvin and Charles D. Pringle. "The Missing Opportunity in Organizational Research: Some Implications for a Theory of Work Performance," *Academy of Management Review* 4 (October 1982): 565.

and knowledge) will be low. Finally, miners who go out on strike illustrate the case of individuals who have the capacity to perform and the opportunity (i.e., management leaves the mine open), yet do not have the requisite willingness; hence, no production occurs. The interaction of the three dimensions necessary for job performance is shown in Figure 1.

The dual arrows indicate that performance is determined by— and partially determines—opportunity, capacity, and willingness. The act of performing, for instance, gives an employee on-the-job experience, which over time may improve that individual's skill or abilities (elements of capacity). High job performance may increase a worker's job satisfaction and reduce his or her anxiety about per- formance (elements of willingness). And one individual's superb performance may inspire his or her co-workers (an element of opportunity) to perform better, which in turn may impel the indi- vidual to even higher performance. (Examples of this can be seen most clearly at athletic events.)

Increasing the opportunity to perform

How can this model help a manager increase the performance level of his subordinates? There is a wealth of literature that focuses on how managers can increase the capacity and willingness of their subordinates. The capacity of subordinates to perform, for instance, can be improved through better recruitment and selection, and by the training and development of subordinates already employed. Willingness to perform can be increased through well-designed incentive and reward systems, improved task designs, and various leadership and motivation techniques already well-known to experienced managers. Virtually overlooked, however, has been the role that opportunity plays in subordinate performance.

If managers are to realize the potential for performance that opportunity provides, they must be made aware that they are responsible for providing a good situation for their subordinates' work. But, how can we provide this good situation?

A good starting point is to *analyze the organization's* (or department's) *technology*. Although state-of-the-art technology often is expensive, and in some fields is subject to rapid change, many organizations fail to assess the opportunity costs incurred in forgoing the latest technology. As a simple example, consider the case of a secretary whose productivity is low and whose work always contains a few errors. The usual "textbook" solutions to such a problem might include any of the following: base some portion of her pay on productivity and error rates; use participative management techniques that allow the secretary to help compose letters or reports, thereby increasing her commitment to their accuracy; give the secretary clearly-stated goals regarding productivity and error rates; or send the secretary to a motivational seminar. In fact, productivity will increase more significantly, and error rates will drop more dramatically, by replacing the secretary's typewriter with a word processor than by any or all of the foregoing suggestions.

Secondly, the manager might *analyze organizational "systems."* For instance, an efficient planning system such as MRP II and CAPP for the delivery of raw materials and parts and for the scheduling of workflow provides better opportunity for higher performance than does an inefficient system. Even willing and capable workers can produce nothing if components are not available when they are needed. Japanese manufacturers, for example, have significantly reduced non-productive "downtime" by perfecting their setup and changeover systems. In reporting on his visit to six Japanese companies earlier in this decade, Robert H. Hayes indicates that while one United States automobile manufacturer took six hours to change the presses in its hood- and fender-stamping department, and Volvo and a German car company each took four hours, Toyota took only twelve minutes.[3] Hence, opportunity can be greatly enhanced by efficient planning and scheduling systems.

The *actions of significant other people* in the organization— apart from traditional leadership and motivation theories—can also increase the opportunity for performance. For instance, personnel policies that result in the hiring and retention of high achievers foster a climate of performance that is likely to affect new employees. It is well known that a person who is around hard-working people is likely to do the same. Placing a willing and capable newcomer in a department that has a climate of high performance, therefore, should benefit that employee's performance. Conversely, placing the same newcomer in a department where the norm is to drink coffee, swap stories, and conduct football pools is likely to adversely impact that employee's performance.

Sponsorship of an aspiring manager by a higher level executive in a *mentor relationship* is a way to affect an individual's performance. With an experienced mentor, the protégé receives valuable advice, introductions to influential people, and the opportunity to develop both management skills and a philosophy of management. A survey of over 400 executives enrolled in Columbia University's Executive Programs revealed that these managers felt that a mentor relationship gave an employee a greater chance to develop his or her abilities, to become stimulated by the mentor's ideas, and to increase in self confidence.[4] An individual with this opportunity is likely to develop into a high job performer more quickly than one who does not.

Still another means of increasing opportunity is through *delegation*. The delegation of challenging and important tasks to promising individuals helps them realize their full potential and pays dividends in high performance. As Edgar H. Schein points out, the difference between a good worker and a poor one may not be a difference in motivation, needs, or ambition. Instead, it might be "more correct to see the good worker as having a boss who provided challenging work while the poor worker had a boss who provided a fragmented and intrinsically meaningless assignment."[5] A manager who delegates increasingly complex assignments to a capable and willing subordinate will not only increase the subordinate's capacity but also provide the opportunity for the subordinate to learn and master new situations. This opportunity should enable the subordinate to perform better and to be better prepared for future promotions.

Finally, some managers can provide the opportunity for a subordinate to perform by *protecting the individual from interruptions and unnecessary meetings*. Northwestern Mutual Life Insurance Company helps its new-business department process more policies by shutting off all incoming calls to the department each Wednesday. On these days, the department processes 23 percent more policies than on other days.[6]

The above suggestions are not meant to be all-inclusive but rather to indicate ways in which managers can increase the opportunity for subordinates to perform. The availability of opportunity can have a dramatic, positive impact on the performance of a promising employee. Managers attempting to improve subordinate performance must carefully create and maintain an environment that encourages and facilitates the highest employee work behavior.

1. For a representative example of each type of theory see, respectively: A. H. Maslow, "A Theory of Human Motivation," *Psychological Review* 50 (1943); 370–396; J. R. Hackman and G. R. Oldham, *Work Redesign* (Reading, Mass.: Addison-Wesley, 1980); V. H. Vroom, *Work and Motivation* (New York: John Wiley & Sons, 1964); and E. A. Locke, "Toward a Theory of Task Motivation and Incentives," *Organizational Behavior and Human Performance* 3 (1968): 157–189.

2. M. Blumberg and C. D. Pringle, "The Missing Opportunity in Organizational Research: Some Implications for a Theory of Work Performance," *Academy of Management Review* 7 (1982): 560–569.

3. R. H. Hayes, "Why Japanese Factories Work," *Harvard Business Review* 59 (July–August, 1981): 59.

4. M. H. Reich, "Executive Views from Both Sides of Mentoring," *Personnel* 62 (March, 1985): 42–46.

5. E. H. Schein, *Organizational Psychology*, 3rd ed. (Englewood Cliffs, N.J.: Prentice-Hall, 1980): 98–99.

6. "Labor Letter," *Wall Street Journal* (October 25, 1985): 1.

An Uneasy Look at Performance Appraisal

Douglas McGregor

Foreword: "Managers are uncomfortable when they are put in the position of 'playing God,'" Douglas McGregor wrote in explaining their resistance to undertaking the conventional kind of appraisal of employee performance. Instead, he advocated an approach in which the subordinate establishes personal short-term goals and evaluates his performance himself. As a consequence, interviews with his manager concentrate on the employee's strengths, rather than his shortcomings, and they tend less to digress into personalities. This article is as pertinent today as when it first appeared in the May–June 1957 issue of HBR [the *Harvard Business Review*]. That its ideas are not as fresh now is testimony to the wide acceptance of McGregor's belief in encouraging individuals to develop their potentialities in the organizational setting. In 1957 he had not yet articulated his famous concepts of Theory X and Theory Y, although the ideas behind them are present in this "HBR Classic."

At the time this article was written, McGregor was Professor of Management at the School of Industrial Management, Massachusetts Institute of Technology. Previously, he had been active in the field of industrial relations and had been President of Antioch College. He died in 1964.

Performance appraisal within management ranks has become standard practice in many companies during the past 20 years and is currently being adopted by many others, often as an important feature of management development programs. The more the method is used, the more uneasy I grow over the unstated assumptions which lie behind it. Moreover, with some searching, I find that a number of people both in education and in industry share my misgivings. This article, therefore, has two purposes:

1. To examine the conventional performance appraisal plan which requires the manager to pass judgment on the personal worth of subordinates.
2. To describe an alternative which places on the subordinate the primary responsibility for establishing performance goals and appraising progress toward them.

Current programs

Formal performance appraisal plans are designed to meet three needs, one for the organization and two for the individual:

1. They provide systematic judgments to back up salary increases, promotions, transfers, and sometimes demotions or terminations.
2. They are a means of telling a subordinate how he is doing, and suggesting needed changes in his behavior, attitudes, skills, or job knowledge; they let him know "where he stands" with the boss.
3. They also are being increasingly used as a basis for the coaching and counseling of the individual by the superior.

Problem of resistance   Personnel administrators are aware that appraisal programs tend to run into resistance from the managers who are expected to administer them. Even managers who admit the necessity of such programs frequently balk at the process—especially the interview part. As a result, some companies do not communicate appraisal results to the individual, despite the general conviction that the subordinate has a right to know his superior's opinion so he can correct his weaknesses.

The boss's resistance is usually attributed to the following causes:

1. A normal dislike of criticizing a subordinate (and perhaps having to argue about it).
2. Lack of skill needed to handle the interviews.
3. Dislike of a new procedure with its accompanying changes in ways of operating.
4. Mistrust of the validity of the appraisal instrument.

To meet this problem, formal controls—scheduling, reminders, and so on—are often instituted. It is common experience that without them fewer than half the appraisal interviews are actually held. But even controls do not necessarily work. Thus:

In one company with a well-planned and carefully administered appraisal program, an opinion poll included two questions regarding appraisals. More than 90% of those answering the questionnaire approved the idea of appraisals. They wanted to know how they stood. Some 40% went on to say that they had never had the experience of being told—yet the files showed that over four fifths of them had signed a form testifying that they had been through an appraisal interview, some of them several times!

The respondents had no reason to lie, nor was there the slightest supposition that their superiors had committed forgery. The probable explanation is that the superiors, being basically resistant to the plan, had conducted the interviews in such a perfunctory manner that many subordinates did not realize what was going on. Training programs designed to teach the skills of appraising and interviewing do help, but they seldom eliminate managerial resistance entirely. The difficulties connected with "negative appraisals" remain a source of genuine concern. There is always some discomfort involved in telling a subordinate he is not doing well. The individual who is "coasting" during the few years prior to retirement after serving his company competently for many years presents a special dilemma to the boss who is preparing to interview him.

Nor does a shift to a form of group appraisal solve the problem. Though the group method tends to have greater validity and, properly administered, can equalize varying standards of judgment, it does not ease the difficulty inherent in the interview. In fact, the superior's discomfort is often intensified when he must base his interview on the results of a *group* discussion of the subordinate's worth. Even if the final judgments have been his, he is not free to discuss the things said by others which may have influenced him.

The underlying cause   What would we think about a method—however valuable for meeting organizational needs—which produces such results in a wide range of companies with a variety of appraisal plans? The problem is one that cannot be dismissed lightly.

Perhaps this intuitive managerial reaction to conventional performance appraisal plans shows a deep but unrecognized wisdom. In my view, it does not reflect anything so simple as resistance to change, or dislike for personnel technique, or lack of skill, or mistrust for rating scales. Rather, managers seem to be expressing real misgivings, which they find difficult to put into words. This could be the underlying cause:

The conventional approach, unless handled with consummate skill and delicacy, constitutes something dangerously close to a violation of the integrity of the personality. Managers are uncomfortable when they are put in the position of "playing God." The respect we hold for the inherent value of the individual leaves us distressed when we must take responsibility for judging the personal worth of a fellow man. Yet the conventional approach to performance appraisal forces us not only to make such judgments and to see them acted upon but also to communicate them to those we have judged. Small wonder we resist!

The modern emphasis upon the manager as a leader who strives to *help* his subordinates achieve both their own and the company's objectives is hardly consistent with the judicial role demanded by most appraisal plans. If the manager must put on his judicial hat occasionally, he does it reluctantly and with understandable qualms. Under such conditions, it is unlikely that the subordinate will be any happier with the results than will the boss. It will not be surprising, either, if he fails to recognize that he has been told where he stands.

Of course, managers cannot escape making judgments about subordinates. Without such evaluations, salary and promotion policies cannot be administered sensibly. But are subordinates like products on an assembly line, to be accepted or rejected as a result of an inspection process? The inspection process may be made more objective or more accurate through research on the appraisal instrument, through training of the "inspectors," or through introducing group appraisal; the subordinate may be "reworked" by coaching or counseling before the final decision to accept or reject him; but as far as the assumptions of the conventional appraisal process are concerned, we still have what is practically identical with a program for product inspection.

On this interpretation, then, resistance to conventional appraisal programs is eminently sound. It reflects an unwillingness to treat human beings like physical objects. The needs of the organization are obviously important, but when they come into conflict with our convictions about the worth and the dignity of the human personality, one or the other must give.

Indeed, by the fact of their resistance managers are saying that the organization must yield in the face of this fundamental human value. And they are thus being more sensitive than are personnel administrators and social scientists whose business it is to be concerned with the human problems of industry!

A new approach

If this analysis is correct, the task before us is clear. We must find a new plan—not a compromise to hide the dilemma, but a bold move to resolve the issue.

A number of writers are beginning to approach the whole subject of management from the point of view of basic social values. Peter Drucker's concept of "management by objectives"[1] offers an unusually promising framework within which we can seek a solution. Several companies, notably General Mills, Incorporated, and General Electric Company, have been exploring different methods of appraisal which rest upon assumptions consistent with Drucker's philosophy.

Responsibility on subordinate   This approach calls on the subordinate to establish short-term performance goals *for himself.* The superior enters the process actively only *after* the subordinate has (*a*) done a good deal of thinking about his job, (*b*) made a careful assessment of his own strengths and weaknesses, and (*c*) formulated some specific plans to accomplish his goals. The superior's role is to help the man relate his self-appraisal, his "targets," and his plans for the ensuing period to the realities of the organization.

The first step in this process is to arrive at a clear statement of the major features of the job. Rather than a formal job description, this is a document drawn up *by the subordinate* after studying the company-approved statement. It defines the broad areas of his responsibility as they actually work out in practice. The boss and employee discuss the draft jointly and modify it as may be necessary until both of them agree that it is adequate.

Working from this statement of responsibilities, the subordinate then establishes his goals or "targets" for a period of, say, six months. These targets are *specific* actions which the man proposes to take, i.e., setting up regular staff meetings to improve communication, reorganizing the office, completing or undertaking a certain study. Thus they are explicitly stated and accompanied by a detailed account of the actions he proposes to take to reach them. This document is, in turn, discussed with the superior and modified until both are satisfied with it.

At the conclusion of the six-month period, the subordinate makes *his own* appraisal of what he has accomplished relative to the targets he had set earlier. He substantiates it with factual data wherever possible. The "interview" is an examination by superior and subordinate together of the subordinate's self-appraisal, and it culminates in a resetting of targets for the next six months.

Of course, the superior has veto power at each step of this process; in an organizational hierarchy anything else would be unacceptable. However, in practice he rarely needs to exercise it. Most subordinates tend to underestimate both their potentialities and their achievements. Moreover, subordinates normally have an understandable wish to satisfy their boss, and are quite willing to adjust their targets or appraisals if the superior feels they are unrealistic. Actually, a much more common problem is to resist the subordinates' tendency to want the boss to tell them what to write down.

Analysis vs. appraisal   This approach to performance appraisal differs profoundly from the conventional one, for it shifts the emphasis from *appraisal* to *analysis*. This implies a more positive approach. No longer is the subordinate being examined by the superior so that his weaknesses may be determined; rather, he is examining himself, in order to define not only his weaknesses but also his strengths and potentials. The importance of this shift of emphasis should not be under-estimated. It is basic to each of the specific differences which distinguish this approach from the conventional one.

The first of these differences arises from the subordinate's new role in the process. He becomes an active agent, not a passive "object." He is no longer a pawn in a chess game called management development.

Effective development of managers does not include coercing them (no matter how benevolently) into acceptance of the goals of the enterprise, nor does it mean manipulating their behavior to suit organizational needs. Rather, it calls for creating a relationship within which a man can take responsibility for developing his own potentialities, plan for himself, and learn from putting his plans into action. In the process, he can gain a genuine sense of satisfaction, for he is utilizing his own capabilities to achieve simultaneously both his objectives and those of the organization. Unless this is the nature of the relationship, "development" becomes a euphemism.

Who knows best?   One of the main differences of this approach is that it rests on the assumption that the individual knows—or can learn—more than anyone else about his own capabilities, needs, strengths and weaknesses, and goals. In the end, only he can determine what is best for his development. The conventional approach, on the other hand, makes the assumption that the superior can know enough about the subordinate to decide what is best for him.

No available methods can provide the superior with the knowledge he needs to make such decisions. Ratings, aptitude and personality tests, and the superior's necessarily limited knowledge of the man's performance yield at best an imperfect picture. Even the most extensive psychological counseling (assuming the superior possesses the competence for it) would not solve the problem because the product of counseling is self-insight on the part of the *counselee.*

(Psychological tests are not being condemned by this statement. On the contrary, they have genuine value in competent hands. Their use by professionals as part of the process of screening applicants for employment does not raise the same questions as their use to "diagnose" the personal worth of accepted members of a management team. Even in the latter instance, the problem under discussion would not arise if test results and interpretations were given to *the individual himself*, to be shared with superiors at his discretion.)

The proper role for the superior, then, is the one that falls naturally to him under the suggested plan: helping the subordinate relate his career planning to the needs and realities of the organization. In the discussions, the boss can use his knowledge of the organization to help the subordinate establish targets and methods for achieving them which will (*a*) lead to increased knowledge and skill, (*b*) contribute to organizational objectives, and (*c*) test the subordinate's appraisal of himself.

This is help which the subordinate wants. He knows well that the rewards and satisfactions he seeks from his career as a manager depend on his contribution to organizational objectives. He is also aware that the superior knows more completely than he what is required for success in this organization and *under this boss*. The superior, then, is the person who can help him test the soundness of his goals and his plans for achieving them. Quite clearly the knowledge and active participation of *both* superior and subordinate are necessary components of this approach.

If the superior accepts this role, he need not become a judge of the subordinate's personal worth. He is not telling, deciding, criticizing, or praising—not "playing God." He finds himself listening, using his own knowledge of the organization as a basis for advising, guiding, encouraging his subordinates to develop their own potentialities. Incidentally, this often leads the superior to important insights about himself and his impact on others.

Looking to the future   Another significant difference is that the emphasis is on the future rather than the past. The purpose of the plan is to establish realistic targets and to seek the most effective ways of reaching them. Appraisal thus becomes a means to a *constructive* end. The 60-year-old "coaster" can be encouraged to set performance goals for himself and to make a fair appraisal of his progress toward them. Even the subordinate who has failed can be helped to consider what moves will be best for himself. The superior rarely finds himself facing the uncomfortable prospect of denying a subordinate's personal worth. A transfer or even a demotion can be worked out without the connotation of a "sentence by the judge."

Performance vs. personality   Finally, the accent is on *performance*, on actions relative to goals. There is less tendency for the personality of the subordinate to become an issue. The superior, instead of finding himself in the position of a psychologist or a therapist, can become a coach helping the subordinate to reach his own decisions on the specific steps that will enable him to reach his targets. Such counseling as may be required demands no deep analysis of the personal motivations or basic adjustment of the subordinate. To illustrate:

Consider a subordinate who is hostile, short-tempered, uncooperative, insecure. The superior need not make any psychological diagnosis. The "target setting" approach naturally directs the subordinate's attention to ways and means of obtaining better interdepartmental collaboration, reducing complaints, winning the confidence of the men under him. Rather than facing the troublesome prospect of forcing his own psychological diagnosis on the subordinate, the superior can, for example, help the individual plan ways of getting "feedback" concerning his impact on his associates and subordinates as a basis for self-appraisal and self-improvement.

There is little chance that a man who is involved in a process like this will be in the dark about where he stands, or that he will forget he is the principal participant in his own development and responsible for it.

A new attitude

As a consequence of these differences we may expect the growth of a different attitude toward appraisal on the part of superior and subordinate alike.

The superior will gain real satisfaction as he learns to help his subordinates integrate their personal goals with the needs of the organization so that both are served. Once the subordinate has worked out a mutually satisfactory plan of action, the superior can delegate to him the responsibility for putting it into effect. He will see himself in a consistent managerial role rather than being forced to adopt the basically incompatible role of either the judge or the psychologist.

Unless there is a basic personal antagonism between the two men (in which case the relationship should be terminated), the superior can conduct these interviews so that both are actively involved in seeking the right basis for constructive action. The organization, the boss, and the subordinate all stand to gain. Under such circumstances the opportunities for learning and for genuine development of both parties are maximal.

The particular mechanics are of secondary importance. The needs of the organization in the administration of salary and promotion policies can easily be met within the framework of the analysis process. The machinery of the program can be adjusted to the situation. No universal list of rating categories is required. The complications of subjective or prejudiced judgment, of varying standards, of attempts to quantify qualitative data, all can be minimized. In fact, *no* formal machinery is required.

Problems of judgment   I have deliberately slighted the many problems of judgment involved in administering promotions and salaries. These are by no means minor, and this approach will not automatically solve them. However, I believe that if we are prepared to recognize the fundamental problem inherent in the conventional approach, ways can be found to temper our present administrative methods.

And if this approach is accepted, the traditional ingenuity of management will lead to the invention of a variety of methods for its implementation. The mechanics of some conventional plans can be adjusted to be consistent with this point of view. Obviously, a program utilizing ratings of the personal characteristics of subordinates would not be suitable, but one which emphasizes *behavior* might be.

Of course, managerial skill is required. No method will eliminate that. This method can fail as readily as any other in the clumsy hands of insensitive or indifferent or power-seeking managers. But even the limited experience of a few companies with this approach indicates that managerial *resistance* is substantially reduced. As a consequence, it is easier to gain the collaboration of managers in developing the necessary skills.

Cost in time   There is one unavoidable cost: the manager must spend considerably more time in implementing a program of this kind. It is not unusual to take a couple of days to work through the initial establishment of responsibilities and goals with each individual. And a periodic appraisal may require several hours rather than the typical 20 minutes.

Reaction to this cost will undoubtedly vary. The management that considers the development of its human resources to be the primary means of achieving the economic objectives of the organization will not be disturbed. It will regard the necessary guidance and coaching as among the most important functions of every superior.

Conclusion

I have sought to show that the conventional approach to performance appraisal stands condemned as a personnel method. It places the manager in the untenable position of judging the personal worth of his subordinates, and of acting on these judgments. No manager possesses, nor could he acquire, the skill necessary to carry out this responsibility effectively. Few would even be willing to accept it if they were fully aware of the implications involved.

It is this unrecognized aspect of conventional appraisal problems which produces the widespread uneasiness and even open resistance of management to appraisals and especially to the appraisal interview.

A sounder approach, which places the major responsibility on the subordinate for establishing performance goals and appraising progress toward them, avoids the major weaknesses of the old plan and benefits the organization by stimulating the development of the subordinate. It is true that more managerial skill and the investment of a considerable amount of time are required, but the greater motivation and the more effective development of subordinates can justify these added costs.

1. See *The Practice of Management* (New York: Harper & Brothers, 1954).

Whither
Performance
Appraisal?

— Neil A. Stroul

Performance appraisal has been a staple in personnel management for over 35 years, but few companies feel comfortable with their systems' effectiveness. Climate surveys and needs analyses routinely expose the inadequacies of performance appraisal systems, and a thriving cottage industry helps organizations improve existing systems or design new ones. Management and staff remain equally indignant about the oppression of the obligatory annual review.

Performance appraisal has come under critical scrutiny at least since 1957, when Douglas McGregor published his classic article "An Uneasy Look at Performance Appraisal" [reprinted in this volume]. In the 30 years since, the flaws McGregor identified persist. Management scientists continue to build on McGregor's criticisms and identify additional problems and solutions.

The "split role" plays an important part in any discussion of performance appraisal systems. Employees see performance feedback from a manager as meaningful when the manager adopts the role of a counselor and sets a helpful tone. But most performance appraisal systems also ask managers to play the role of judge, evaluating the individual's performance for purposes of salary administration, promotability, and so forth. The two roles are inherently incompatible; to the extent that the manager serves as a judge, the effectiveness of the feedback is diminished. Performance appraisal effectiveness rests on managers' abilities to separate the two roles.

Another factor compromising performance appraisal: the individual and the organization naturally have very different goals. In theory, performance appraisal serves a dual purpose: as a control mechanism to monitor performance and goal attainment and as a feedback mechanism to foster individual growth and development. In practice, however, only the first purpose is served.

Internal conflicts explain this gap between theory and reality. For example, the organizational goal of using performance appraisal to develop employees through counseling, coaching, and career planning conflicts with another avowed goal to seek information on which to base rewards and personnel decisions. In turn, there are major conflicts between the organization's wish to collect information to make personnel decisions and the employee's wish to seek important rewards and to maintain self-esteem. And these employee needs sometimes conflict with the organization's goals for employee development. It's not hard to understand why performance appraisal often elicits tension, defensiveness, and avoidance for both managers and staff.

Designing performance appraisal systems

Two prevalent solutions try to resolve these conflicts:

1. Systems that recognize the competing priorities of individuals and organizations and attempt to alleviate conflicts through intelligent design
2. Management training that emphasizes the importance of providing staff with ongoing feedback, developing interpersonal skills to foster effective staff relationships, and developing interviewing and problem-solving skills for effectively conducting performance evaluations and reviews.

Most efforts at designing intelligent performance appraisal systems separate the manager's roles of judge and counselor by encouraging two interviews. For the organization's need to monitor and control performance and to make rational personnel decisions, each employee participates in a *performance review*. The focus is on accomplishments, goal attainment, and successes and failures. Here the manager acts as a judge. Salary adjustments and other personnel decisions rely on the results of the performance review.

Some other time, the manager and employee go through a *development review*. Here, they focus on strengths and weaknesses, career aspirations, and a training or development plan.

But some managers dislike the performance appraisal process so much that they resist doing two separate interviews. Personnel expert David Wight suggests a single interview that evolves over four discrete phases.

Phase I: As a counselor, the manager reviews performance with the employee in a nonevaluative manner. The emphasis is strictly on providing feedback.

Phase II: The manager evaluates performance. While this

phase may repeat points from Phase I, the purpose and tone are different because the manager must judge performance—as concretely as possible.

Phase III: The manager provides the employee with an overall rating and links this evaluation to any salary adjustments. While the manager's intent is not to justify or defend, he or she should explain how the rating was calculated.

Phase IV: The manager links current performance to future options, discusses the various incentives, and initiates planning for the next review.

To successfully employ this model, the manager must develop the sensitivity and interpersonal competence to cope with emotional issues that may arise. While the four-phase approach recognizes the manager's judge-counselor conflict, it implicitly reinforces the manager's hierarchical position and offers no concrete suggestions for establishing a collaborative dialogue.

Several measures can foster collaboration. For instance, managers might use two separate appraisal forms: one for evaluation, which becomes part of the personnel record, and one for development, which does not. The appraisal process can also rely on a combination of management-by-objectives and behavioral measures to assess performance or employ separate assessments of performance and potential. Another unique approach combines managers' assessments of employees and employees' assessments of managers. Other systems incorporate employee self-appraisals or use different formats for different employees.

Other flexible systems use different performance appraisals for different populations. In 1985 *Personnel Administrator* highlighted a performance appraisal system developed by John Oliver that classifies all jobs into four major categories: hierarchical positions, professional positions, entrepreneurial or task positions, and sociotechnical or group-job designs. The particulars of performance appraisal—standards, forms, and procedures—vary for each group.

For example, in hierarchical positions, jobs are narrowly defined, discretion is minimal, and authority and direction are vested in the supervisor. Therefore performance appraisal is essentially a control mechanism to be implemented using a top-down approach. Supervisors set the standards and all communication channels through them.

Performance appraisal for professional positions largely involves compliance with the goals, duties, ethics, and standards of conduct as proclaimed by professional associations. As a result, standards reflect an integration of position-specific accountabilities and professional practices. Training and career development seeks to improve professional competence.

Task positions, such as entrepreneurial or sales jobs have re-

1. Who sets the performance standards?
2. What form should the standards take?
3. How do we decide what is reasonable but challenging?
4. How many standards are needed to measure overall performance?
5. How much weight should each criterion (standard) carry in the overall performance judgment?
6. How are the standards communicated?
7. Are there hidden irrational criteria that take precedence over the valid rational criteria? If so, how can this problem be solved?
8. What measures will be used?
9. What is the measurement level of these measures (quantitative or qualitative)?
10. Who provides the performance measure?
11. Are the performance measures objective enough or too subjective to be acceptable?
12. When and how will measurements be made?
13. How often will measures be compared to the standard?
14. Will the frequency have a positive or adverse affect on satisfaction or productivity?
15. How often will the staff member be rated?
16. How often will the rating be communicated to the staff member?
17. Who will rate the staff member's performance?
18. Who will communicate the rating to the staff member?
19. How can the staff member improve performance?
20. How can the organization aid in improving the staff member's performance?
21. How can the organization ensure that objective performance ratings are used in decision making instead of subjective, informal, irrational, or irrelevant ratings?

Figure 1. Oliver's 21 questions to ask.

wards and punishments built into the work itself. Rewards are based on successful completion of the goal or task. Performance appraisals thus function as goal-setting sessions designed to bolster achievement and motivation. An MBO approach using joint goal-setting works effectively.

Group-job designs are characterized by employees organized in teams where each team member has comparable responsibilities. A democratic process involving all team members sets the standards. Since sharing of responsibilities is common, there should be several standards, but realistically no one should be expected to excel in all of them. Performance appraisal weighs standards involving establishing effective working relationships, group problem-solving, and so forth.

Figure 1 shows 21 questions that John Oliver, in a 1985 *Personnel Journal* article, says designers of performance appraisal sys-

1. *Are managers rewarded for developing subordinates?* In many organizations, developing subordinates is either not rewarded or inadvertently punished.
2. *Do managers receive skill training and assistance in using the system and, specifically, in being helpers or counselors?* Often, managers are only given the actual appraisal form and cursory instructions for completing the forms. Managers need training in rating performance objectively and in problem-solving and helping skills.
3. *Are job descriptions or specific job-goal documents based on behavioral or job-relevant standards?* Recent legal rulings suggest that performance appraisals are comparable to selection tests, and therefore must be demonstrably related to job content.
4. *Are employees actively involved in the appraisal process?* Generally, systems that incorporate end-user input function more effectively.
5. *Does mutual goal setting take place?* Research evidence suggests that joint goal setting is related to performance improvement and improved organizational climate.
6. *Do appraisal sessions have a problem solving focus?* A problem solving focus is essential for performance improvement.
7. *Is the judge role clearly separated from the helper-counselor role?* This is a key issue that is often thwarted because of difficulty in implementation.
8. *Does the paperwork and technical assistance required by the appraisal system place an unreasonable work load on the manager?* This is often overlooked but is a key determinant of success or failure.
9. *Are peer comparisons a central feature of the appraisal process?* Peer comparison is a popular notion that can often lead to devastating results.
10. *Is information needed for administrative action accessible and effectively used?* This is another feature too often overlooked in designing a successful performance appraisal system.

Figure 2. Sashkin's 10 "heuristics."

tems must answer in order to develop effective forms and procedures. Marshall Sashkin, in a 1981 *Organizational Dynamics* article, identified 10 heuristics or rules of thumb for assessing the effectiveness of a performance appraisal system. Figure 2 lists them.

The works of Oliver and Sashkin both suggest that performance appraisal's troubled history stems from several problems: vague and conflicting goals, managers' competing roles, inappropriate procedures for target populations, inadequate support systems, insufficient time to appraise performance properly, and failure to reward managers for appraising performance or developing staff.

Performance appraisal's position
The positioning of performance appraisal within the organization also contributes to performance appraisal's precarious situation.

When performance appraisal originally gained widespread acceptance, it made sense in the context of prevailing management philosophies and market conditions. Demographics supported a work force of fairly uniform composition. The United States was the dominant commercial force in the world, resources were abundant, inflation was minimal, and markets could be divided into two categories: those already entered and those yet to be entered. American industry was built upon manufacturing, technology produced improvements rather than revolutions, and the general state of the economy was robust. Steady, if unspectacular growth made stability commonplace. Organizational efforts to exert control surprised few employees, although they could have resisted. By and large, a work force characterized by shared values and goals felt that performance appraisal was a necessary evil, even if it was unavoidably stifling. In this context performance appraisal became entrenched as a control mechanism.

Individuals who had worked their way up the organizational ladder filled the ranks of middle management. Based on their experience with other managers, they intuitively identified preferred management behaviors, adopting them as their own. Where training was available, they acquired additional concepts and techniques. But by and large corporate culture transmitted values, expectations, and beliefs through successive generations of managers.

So it is today with performance appraisal. Because management practices are linked to the past through corporate culture, most managers still define their roles in the traditional terms of planning and controlling. As a result, performance appraisal has become institutionalized as a control mechanism rather than as a tool for development—even though each generation found it unpleasant. Managers sometimes discuss performance appraisal as a development tool, but this function rarely gets the emphasis accorded controlling aspects.

It's a shame too, because changing peoples' mindsets—not revising evaluation forms—is the key to successful performance appraisal. Performance appraisal as a developmental tool requires managers to adopt a different, nontraditional role. Training managers in performance appraisal in an additive fashion—where all managers receive stand-alone performance appraisal training that teaches the intricacies of the system—is insufficient.

Repositioning the manager's role

Instead, basic supervisory and management training must establish managers' roles as developers of people. Training and cultural norms must define and reinforce managers' responsibility to bring out the best in the people who report to them.

Most management models emphasize the manager's role in

managing performance. Situational leadership, for example, asks managers to assess employees' maturity levels—their willingness and ability to meet various job demands. Depending upon the individual's maturity level, which in turn depends on the results expected, the manager selects a management style. While situational leadership yields several effective management principles, it is essentially a status quo management model with a primary focus of helping the manager control performance. For performance appraisal, this type of training is not enough.

Effective management training helps managers answer these questions:

1. Do I want to be a manager? How do I feel about guiding or directing others' work? How do I feel about monitoring, problem solving, arbitrating, and the like? What am I willing to do to be an effective manager?
2. What am I doing to earn my staff's respect? Do they perceive me as a capable technician and manager? Does my staff believe that I appreciate and look out for their best interests?
3. Do I really understand what is going on here? Are goals clear, job descriptions articulated, standards in place? Am I sufficiently informed that I can make knowledgeable assessments about the success and failure of my staff members' goal attainments?
4. What am I doing to keep abreast of my staff's performance? Am I aware of available resources, the obstacles and difficulties they encounter, their skill deficiencies and strengths? Do I know what factors affect performance? Do I collect information through firsthand experience?
5. Can I provide constructive feedback and jointly seek solutions to performance problems? Do I have hidden agendas? Do I really want to help? Is my goal to bring out the best in my staff?
6. To bring out the best in each staff member, what must I do?

Redefining managers' roles

To bring out the best in staff, managers need a broad frame of reference in which they manage performance *and* development. Managers must shift their perspective and define their role in a new way, namely managing each employee's learning curve. This frame of reference goes by the name of *adaptive managing*. Figure 3 graphically displays the various responsibilities implicit in adaptive managing.

When managers focus on each employee's learning curve, they focus on both performance and development. This emphasis on

Figure 3. Adaptive managing.

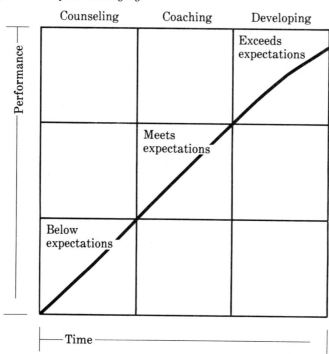

learning clearly indicates that when employee performance meets expectations, managers must do more than merely maintain it through monitoring and control. Managers use different strategies depending on whether the employee performs below, at, or above expected levels. In adaptive managing, achieving results becomes a baseline at the point where employee performance meets expectations. At that point managers must encourage and foster growth to help employees reach their potential.

Adaptive managing thus requires a dual-time orientation that looks at the present and the future. Managers have to estimate the developmental level for each staff member by determining the extent to which staff members currently meet expectations and to what extent they're realizing their potential. The assessment process, shown in Figure 4, uses a series of questions and answers to help managers do this.

Traditional top-down, control-motivated performance appraisal may be appropriate to resolve a performance deficiency, but lasting performance improvement happens only if managers can enlist employee support and input in the problem-solving process. The adaptive managing model provides a structure and process for obtaining such support and input.

In the adaptive managing model, managers counsel employees to resolve performance problems. In coaching, the employee's performance is acceptable, but indicators suggest that the person has

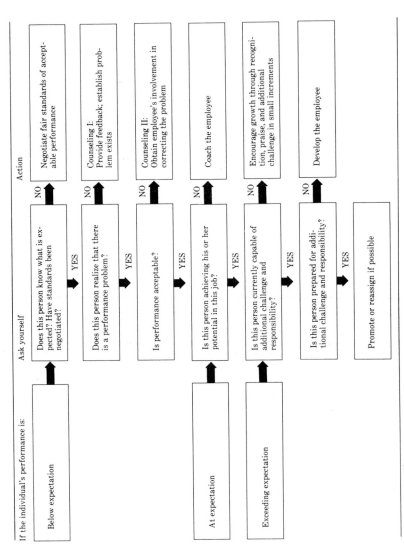

Figure 4   The assessment process.

the potential to accomplish more. The manager must develop a strategy to help this person grow and reach a level of performance that regularly exceeds expectations. In developing, the employee's performance consistently exceeds expectations, and the manager must devise a strategy to incorporate into the employee's position greater challenge or prepare her or him for a new position involving greater challenge and responsibility.

When counseling employees who perform below expectations, managers both initiate and drive the intervention. That's not the case when employees already perform acceptably. A manager can only rightfully demand that an employee perform acceptably. Consequently, the manager may initiate coaching or development, but the staff member must drive it. In other words, while counseling is collaborative, the manager is in control. In coaching and developing the employee, as the driving force, must share control.

The repositioning of performance appraisal thus hinges on redefining the manager's role. Managers must not only adopt a new frame of reference—managing learning; they must also share control. Managers will only agree to this redefinition if it will help them meet their objectives. Training is an important vehicle for obtaining managerial support.

Training's role

The ultimate success or failure of a performance appraisal system rests on the training effort that supports it. To successfully support performance appraisal, training must fulfill the following three functions:

1. Reposition the manager's role and emphasize staff development as an essential responsibility
2. Help managers develop skills and strategies to enact their new role
3. Give managers the technology they need to apply in their staff development activities. Managers must be able to apply training concepts and tools as necessary without depending on the training function.

Performance appraisal training typically takes the form of stand-alone seminars or workshops. In addition to reviewing forms and procedures, content generally includes providing staff with ongoing feedback and deciding when and how it should be delivered. These seminars also focus on building sound interviewing and problem-solving skills and developing interpersonal competence that fosters effective staff relationships.

This approach may work when an organization installs a new performance appraisal system with an existing work force. But after the first wave this type of training tends to reinforce performance appraisal as a control mechanism. Performance appraisal becomes just a tool, much like a microcomputer, because this training emphasizes techniques instead of fundamental role changes. The performance appraisal system itself, rather than the manager, becomes the agent for developing staff. Forms, rating scales, appraisal schedules, and documentation take precedence over the staff member's growth. Relationship variables like rapport, trust, and goodwill fade into the background.

Training must emphasize performance appraisal as a natural outgrowth of the manager's role. Staff development—bringing out the best in people—must receive as much emphasis as controlling, monitoring, and delegating. The training must help managers acquire the skills necessary to successfully enact the role. Because successful staff development requires the manager to collaborate instead of rely on hierarchical authority, training must help managers confidently share power. Managers must understand that sharing power neither erodes authority nor compromises results. The adaptive managing model is particularly useful in this context, because it clearly demonstrates that only staff members who achieve acceptable results are ready for coaching and development.

The collaboration between managers and employees in coaching and developing sometimes seems one-sided. The manager merely supports; actual growth depends on the employee's commitment. As a coach and developer, the manager must work from the sidelines; in fact, too much input and activity from the manager potentially could have an adverse effect. A key goal in coaching and development must be to help the employee assume greater challenges and responsibility, a goal incompatible with excessive dependence upon the manager.

Some managers are less than eager to assume the role of coach and developer because they feel they don't have coaching and development skills. Performance appraisal training can instill necessary confidence by teaching feedback, interpersonal effectiveness, interviewing, and problem-solving techniques.

Training can also contribute to managers' becoming developers by making training technology user-friendly so they use it to develop their own staffs. Case studies, skills inventories, basic work redesign techniques, and cross-training principles all represent training activities that managers can use. Performance appraisal training should teach these techniques. Trainers can also prepare a handbook reviewing organizational policies concerning job rotation, tuition reimbursements, and internal and external training resources.

When performance appraisal training teaches managers how to teach their staffs, it reinforces the notion that staff development is an essential managerial function.

Performance Appraisal and the Law

━━━━━━━━━ Shelley R. Burchett and Kenneth P. De Meuse

Performance appraisal may be informal or impromptu—when, for example, a group of managers discuss their employees' performance at a staff meeting. Or it may be formal and systematic—when, for example, an organization develops written appraisal instruments that are used at specific and regular intervals. In either case, the conclusions reached about employee performance can impact various personnel decisions: Data may be used to determine merit-pay increase, promotion, participation in training and development activities, retention, layoff, referral, demotion, transfer, or discharge.

If performance evaluations are used to make these types of decisions, the development, implementation, and utilization of evaluation instruments become important legal issues. When used in such personnel decisions, performance appraisal falls under the general rubric of an employee-selection activity and consequently under the dictates of the *Uniform Guidelines on Employee Selection Procedures* (U.S. Government Printing Office, 1978). For example, an employee may be *selected* for a merit-pay increase based on a high performance-evaluation score, or *selected* for discharge based on a low performance-evaluation score. While there has been an increased awareness among employers in the last 15 years of the necessity of selecting employees fairly, many organizations still regard "selection" as the decision to hire or not to hire. This is a mistake. Post-employment decisions like the ones listed above also involve selection. Failure to adhere to the *Uniform Guidelines* (and related laws) when making such decisions can result in costly litigation and reinstatement with back-pay awards.

Reprinted, by permission of the publisher, from PERSONNEL, July 1985, © 1985 American Management Association, New York. All rights reserved.

This article reviews the legal requirements and concerns applicable to performance appraisal: relevant constitutional and statutory laws and relevant court decisions (case law). Some specific suggestions on how to establish a legally defensible performance-appraisal system are also presented.

Constitutional and statutory law

Although federal regulation of employment practices is provided by the U.S. Constitution, detailed regulation of employee-selection and performance-appraisal procedures is relatively recent. Not until

Exhibit 1. Laws impacting performance appraisal.

Law	Effect	Enforcement agency
Article 1, U.S. Constitution, 1779	Congress regulates practices affecting commerce.	U.S. Congress
Title VII, Civil Rights Act, 1964	Discrimination on the basis of race, color, religion, sex, or national origin in employment practice is unlawful.	Equal Employment Opportunity Commission
Executive Orders 11246 and 11375, 1965 and 1967	Discrimination on the basis of race, color, religion, sex, or national origin in the employment practices of federal agencies, departments, contractors and subcontractors is unlawful.	Office of Federal Contracts Compliance Programs
Age Discrimination in Employment Act, 1967 and 1978	Employers are prohibited from discriminating on the basis of age (applies to persons between the ages of 40 and 70).	Equal Employment Opportunity Commission
Rehabilitation Act, 1973 and 1974	Discrimination on the basis of handicap in federally funded programs is prohibited.	Office of Federal Contracts Compliance Programs
Pregnancy Discrimination Act, 1978	Title VII is amended so that discrimination includes a prohibition against discrimination in employment on the basis of pregnancy.	Equal Employment Opportunity Commission

1964 was a broad, far-reaching civil rights act specifically addressing illegal discrimination passed. Since then, several additional antidiscrimination laws have been passed. (See Exhibit 1.)

United States Constitution   Article I, Section 8 of the U.S. Constitution grants Congress the power to regulate commerce among the states. Commerce refers to the exchange of goods or property of any kind or to the transportation of people or property. Thus the U.S. Constitution gives Congress the legal foundation to enact future laws prohibiting employment practices that impede interstate commerce. This power was upheld by the United States Supreme Court in *Heart of Atlanta Motel, Incorporated* v. *United States*,[1] which prohibited the motel from excluding blacks, since the motel's policy obstructed interstate commerce.

Civil Rights Act of 1964   On July 2, the U.S. Congress passed the Civil Rights Act of 1964. Title VII of that act states:

It shall be an unlawful employment practice for an employer: (a) to fail or refuse to hire or to discharge any individual, or otherwise discriminate against any individual with respect to his compensation, terms, conditions, or privileges of employment because of such individual's race, color, religion, sex, or national origin, or (b) to limit, segregate, or classify his employees or applicants in any way which would deprive or tend to deprive any individual of employment opportunities or to otherwise adversely affect his status as an employee, because of such individual's race, color, religion, sex, or national origin.

Title VII specifically prohibits discrimination by employers, public and private employment agencies, labor organizations, and joint labor-management apprenticeship programs.

Title VII of the Civil Rights Act is administered by the Equal Employment Opportunity Commission (EEOC). The EEOC may investigate charges of employment discrimination and bring suit in the federal courts against employers on behalf of aggrieved individuals. The EEOC is also responsible for disseminating timely guidelines interpreting Title VII. In 1972, the powers of the EEOC were extended to include federal, state, and municipal employees as well as employees of educational institutions. Before this date, the EEOC had no jurisdiction over employment practices in the public sector.

Executive Orders 11246 and 11375   Executive Order 11246 was issued in 1965 and amended in 1967 by Executive Order 11375. These two executive orders ban discrimination on the basis of race, color, religion, sex, or national origin in the employment practices of all federal agencies and departments as well as in the employment practices of federal contractors and subcontractors. The executive orders are more stringent than Title VII, because they require that each organization employing 100 or more individuals maintain a written affirmative action program with goals and timetables. These executive orders require that whenever job categories include fewer women or minorities than would be reasonably expected (according to their availability in the labor market), the employer must establish numerical goals for increasing their number in those categories. These goals must include probable dates for attainment (timetables). The EEOC monitors compliance with these orders for public employers. The Office of Federal Contract Compliance Programs (OFCCP), an agency within the Department of Labor, monitors compliance of contractors and subcontractors.

Age Discrimination in Employment Act of 1967 (amended in 1978) The Age Discrimination Act of 1967, as amended in 1978, prohibits employers from discriminating on the basis of a person's age. All employees at or between the ages of 40 and 70 are protected by this act. Certain groups, for example, law-enforcement officers and firefighters, are exempted from the law's provisions based on the belief that public safety might be jeopardized if older workers were in these positions. This act is also administered by the EEOC.

Rehabilitation Act of 1973 (amended in 1974) The Rehabilitation Act prohibits federally funded programs from discriminating against handicapped persons. The scope of this act is similar to the scope of Executive Orders 11246 and 11375, since it applies to public and private employers contracting work from the federal government. Parties subject to the provisions of this act are expected to include qualified handicapped workers in the applicant and promotion pools. As with the executive orders, the OFCCP is designated to monitor compliance.

Pregnancy Discrimination Act of 1978 Congress passed the Pregnancy Discrimination Act to amend Title VII. The Pregnancy Act amends the definition of sex discrimination to include discrimination in employment on the basis of pregnancy, childbirth, or related medical conditions. This act protects female employees against being fired or refused a job or promotion merely because they are pregnant or have undergone an abortion. Furthermore, if other employees who take disability leave are entitled to get their jobs back when they are physically able to work again, so are women who have been unable to work because of pregnancy. In essence, the Pregnancy Act requires employers to extend equal treatment to women affected by pregnancy in all terms, conditions, and rights of employment, which includes receipt of benefits under employee benefits programs.

Uniform Guidelines on Employee Selection Procedures

In addition to the laws summarized in Exhibit 1, the *Uniform Guidelines* have essentially gained the force of law. When Congress passed the Civil Rights Act of 1964, it explicitly authorized the use of any professionally developed ability test as long as it was not designed, intended, or used to discriminate.

In an attempt to interpret and clarify how testing could satisfy the requirements of the law under Title VII, the EEOC and the Department of Labor released guidelines in 1966 and 1968, respectively. Their view was that if a test had an adverse impact (screened out a higher proportion of minorities or females than white males), then it was illegal unless it was used because of business necessity. In 1971, the Supreme Court upheld that even if discrimination is unintentional, employment tests that have an adverse impact and cannot be justified as a business necessity are still in violation of Title VII. (See *Griggs* v. *Duke Power Company*.[2]) The EEOC and Department of Labor guidelines were subsequently combined into the *Uniform Guidelines on Employee Selection Procedures* in 1978. Two other government agencies, the Civil Service Commission and the Department of Justice, also adopted these guidelines in 1978.

The *Uniform Guidelines* do not apply only to written tests; they cover all selection procedures that are used in making employment decisions. They apply to preemployment and postemployment practices. Therefore, the *Uniform Guidelines* are clearly applicable to performance evaluations when the results of these evaluations are used in making employment decisions.

Since 1971, the *Guidelines* have been the authoritative source for requirements of employment testing. It appears that the primary objective of the *Guidelines* is to require employers to demonstrate that their tests measure the behaviors necessary for successful on-the-job performance whenever such tests disproportionately screen out particular groups. The courts have generally judged the legality of employment procedures under Title VII according to the principles laid out by the *Guidelines*.

Additional laws

There are several other federal anti-discrimination laws: the Fifth, Thirteenth, and Fourteenth Amendments to the U.S. Constitution, the Civil Rights Acts of 1866 and 1871, and the Equal Pay Act of 1963. In addition, various state laws essentially mirror the provisions of Title VII and prohibit discrimination in employment by smaller employers who may not be liable under Title VII. These laws are not usually relevant to the legality of performance appraisal. Most complaints about performance appraisal involve vi-

Exhibit 2.   *A summary of court cases and significant rulings.* *

Case	Year	Court	Prevailing party	Significant rulings
Griggs v. Duke Power Company	1971	Supreme	Employee	EEOC guidelines first endorsed. Adverse impact requires demonstration of job-relatedness. Employer intent to discriminate irrelevant.
Marquez v. Omaha District Sales Office, Ford Division of the Ford Motor Company	1971	Appeals, 8th Circuit	Employee	Documentation necessary. Misuse of legal appraisal system may violate Title VII.
Rowe v. General Motors	1972	Appeals, 5th Circuit	Employee	Lack of appraiser training condemned. Subjective performance standards condemned. Communication of performance standards required.
Harper v. Mayor and City Council of Baltimore	1972	District	Employee	Neutral results may indicate discrimination. Consistent evaluation dimensions required.
Brito v. Zia Company	1973	Appeals, 10th Circuit	Employee	Performance appraisals are "employment tests." Adverse impact requires demonstration of validity of appraisal system. Objective performance standards should supplement subjective standards. Standardized administration and scoring of appraisals required.

Case	Year	Court	Favored	Findings
Wade v. Mississippi Cooperative Extension Service	1974	District	Employee	Job analysis required. Appraisal on general traits condemned.
Albemarle Paper Company v. Moody	1975	Supreme	Employee	Appraisals as criteria must be job-related. Endorsement of EEOC guidelines regarding criterion development.
Patterson v. American Tobacco Company	1978	Appeals, 4th Circuit	Employee	Job analysis necessary. Objective performance standards required.
Zell v. United States	1979	District	Organization	Regular evaluations supported. Job-related standards demonstrated. Performance standards properly communicated.
Ramirez v. Hofheinz	1980	Appeals, 5th Circuit	Organization	Subjective performance standards supported. Past record of employer important.
Turner v. State Highway Commission of Missouri	1982	District	Organization	Documentation complete.
Carpenter v. Stephen F. Austin State University	1983	Appeals, 5th Circuit	Employee	Updated job analysis. Performance standards required to be demonstrably job-related. Appraiser training required.

*For a complete synopsis of these cases, write to Kenneth De Meuse, Intergraph Corporation, One Madison Industrial Park, Huntsville, Alabama 35807.

olations of rights directly provided by Title VII. Title VII, without a doubt, affords the most broad and sweeping prohibitions against discrimination in employment.

Case law

Exhibit 2 presents the significant rulings of 12 major court cases involving performance-appraisal practices. These cases are representative of numerous other cases that have been litigated during the past 15 years. The cases reviewed here are significant to the legal assessment of employees and/or address some issue not dealt with previously by the courts. Taken together, these cases give a picture of the characteristics that courts specifically investigate when scrutinizing performance-appraisal systems.

Role of job analysis   The courts have repeatedly condemned the use of performance-evaluation instruments that have not been developed from a systematic analysis of the job. In a landmark case *Albemarle Paper Company* v. *Moody*,[3] the Albemarle Company's ranking instrument had not been developed from an analysis of the job, and supervisors had not been given specific directions about how to rank employees; furthermore, employees were ranked together, irrespective of their job duties. The court noted that there was no way of knowing what aspects of performance supervisors were evaluating, or whether they were even evaluating the same aspects of performance. In *Wade* v. *Mississippi Cooperative Extension Service*,[4] a statewide service organization was found in violation of Title VII because the appraisal instrument was not derived from a job analysis. Similarly, the court reiterated the job-analysis directive in *Patterson* v. *American Tobacco Company*.[5] In the case of *Carpenter* v. *Stephen F. Austin State University*,[6] the university was chastised by the court for using obsolete job descriptions in evaluating its employees. Consequently, periodic job analysis also seems to be important.

Focus on work behaviors and objective performance measures   The *Uniform Guidelines* clearly specify (and the courts have generally upheld) that employee evaluation should concentrate on job-specific behaviors rather than on potentially relevant traits, abilities, and psychological characteristics. In the early 1970s, the courts ruled that such aspects as appearance, ethical habits, and loyalty are vague and subjective and may not have any impact on job performance (*Brito* v. *Zia Company*[7]). The courts, however, have not forbidden the use of subjective supervisory ratings altogether. In a recent case, the court agreed that the Houston Police Department may use subjective judgment in deciding on qualification for a position (*Ramirez* v. *Hofheinz*[8]). In general, the courts have looked favorably on subjective evaluations when they are supplemented by more objective, behavioral measures of performance (see *Zell* v. *United States*[9]).

Communication of performance standards   Courts have reacted negatively to performance-evaluation systems when standards have not been communicated to employees. For example, in *Rowe* v. *General Motors*,[10] the court ruled that one of the discriminatory aspects of the motor company's performance-appraisal policy was that criteria on which promotions were based were not clearly communicated to hourly employees. In contrast, the court more recently decided that a performance-appraisal system was legal, because (among other things) employees were explicitly informed of the standards on which they would be evaluated (*Zell* v. *United States*). In this case, Dr. Zell was a chemist for the federal government who claimed that, because of her age, she was not promoted. The government countered: She was evaluated regularly; evaluation dimensions were job-relevant (patients, publications, and awards); Zell was aware of those standards; and she had consistently received lower evaluation scores than her promoted colleagues. The court agreed with the federal government. Therefore, the communication of clear, specific performance standards is essential in any performance-appraisal system.

Supervisory training   Training supervisors to properly evaluate employees seems to be an important consideration in avoiding legal problems. For example, in *Carpenter* v. *Stephen F. Austin State University* the court ordered the development of written, objective guidelines to assist supervisors in making promotion (and hiring) decisions. In *Rowe* v. *General Motors*, the court noted that without some sort of evaluation guidelines, it was impossible to determine whether employees were being judged by the same criteria. In *Harper* v. *Mayor and City Council of Baltimore*,[11] the court pointed out the necessity of using the same criteria to evaluate all employees.

Role of documentation   One of the most important considerations in a legally defensible performance-appraisal system is documentation. Reasons for personnel evaluations (and subsequent actions) must be properly recorded in writing if employers are to adequately defend themselves in the courts. In *Marquez* v. *Omaha District Sales Office, Ford Division of the Ford Motor Company*,[12] the court found the company guilty of racial discrimination when it could not document its reason for removing an employee from a promotion list. Conversely, the court recently ruled in favor of a company's decision not to promote an employee because the personnel file contained specific instances of inadequate performance (*Turner* v. *State Highway Commission of Missouri*[13]).

Monitoring the performance appraisal system   In 1972, the courts indicated that appraisal procedures should contain safeguards for avoiding discriminatory practices (*Rowe* v. *General Motors*). At a minimum, a formal appeal mechanism that employees can use to question perceived unfair ratings should be provided. In 1983, the court also made it clear that appraisal systems must be updated as job responsibilities change (*Carpenter* v. *Stephen F. Austin State University*). Both of the above cases stress the need to continually monitor and review one's performance-appraisal procedures.

Summary of case law   The case-law review indicates several trends. Most important, the courts have, by and large, closely adhered to the principles in the *Uniform Guidelines* as well as previous guidelines on employee-selection procedures. The courts have required job analysis, focused on work-related behaviors, insisted on documentation, and so forth. The review also reveals that essential issues involved in performance appraisal (for example, job-relatedness and documentation) were addressed in the early 1970s (*Marquez* and *Brito*), and subsequent cases affirmed these principles (*Zell*, *Turner*, and *Carpenter*).

Exhibit 2 indicates that organizations have been winning challenges to their appraisal systems more often in recent years than in previous years. Perhaps organizations are becoming more sophisticated in their appraisal techniques and more aware of the legal ramifications of poorly designed appraisal systems.

It is worth noting that only two of the cases reviewed here (*Griggs* and *Albemarle*) are Supreme Court cases. The remainder are circuit and district courts cases. Employers and employees should recognize that decisions of circuit and district courts do not have the same finality or force of consensus as Supreme Court decisions. While it is theoretically possible for evaluation practices deemed acceptable by these courts to be ruled illegal by future Supreme Court decisions, it is highly unlikely, given the consistency of lower court rulings.

Guidelines for a legally defensible performance appraisal

If the EEOC decides to challenge an organization's performance-appraisal process, there is very little the employer can do. Because the technology of performance appraisal is not well developed and because there is bound to be error in human evaluation, it is impossible to design an appraisal system that is completely "safe" from litigation at this time. However, by examining performance-appraisal procedures in light of the statutory and case law, an employer can reduce the likelihood of being found guilty of discrimination.

The *Uniform Guidelines* say: "The relevance of criteria and their freedom from bias are of particular concern when there are significant differences in measures of job performance for different groups." Consequently, it is especially important that an organization's performance-appraisal system be well-developed, valid, and reliable when minority employees are evaluated lower than their majority counterparts. This does not imply that all is legally acceptable when both groups are assessed equally. The courts are also concerned that job decisions such as promotions, transfers, and so forth, are based on those appraisals. Moreover, employee evaluations that accurately reflect job performance are fair to the employee and will likely increase the efficiency of company operations.

A review of the law points to several policies organizations should follow in increasing the accuracy and appropriateness of performance-appraisal procedures and decreasing the probability of legal action.

1. *Analyze the job to ascertain characteristics important to successful performance.*
2. *Incorporate these characteristics into a rating instrument.* The characteristics should be specific and behaviorally anchored. General skills, abilities, and personality traits are criteria that should be avoided. Objective performance measures (for example, absenteeism or tardiness) should be used to supplement subjective performance measures when possible.
3. *Communicate performance standards to employees.*
4. *Train supervisors to use the rating instrument.* At a minimum, provide all raters with written instructions about the proper use of the instrument as well as with written criteria upon which raters are to base their judgments.
5. *Document evaluations and reasons for subsequent personnel actions.*
6. *Monitor the performance-appraisal system.* Formally review work-performance behaviors and output measures periodically to ensure that they have not become irrelevant or obsolete. Provide a formal appeal mechanism for employees who wish to question ratings.

The above evaluation guidelines may not prevent EEOC litigation, but they will provide employers with firm evidence to legally defend their appraisal practices.

1. Heart of Atlanta Motel, Incorporated v. United States (379 U. S. 241 [1964]).
2. Griggs v. Duke Power Company (401 U.S. 424 [1971]).
3. Albemarle Paper Company v. Moody (422 U.S. 405 [1975]).
4. Wade v. Mississippi Cooperative Extension Service (372 F.Supp. 126 [1974]).
5. Patterson v. American Tobacco Company (586 F2d 300 [1978]).
6. Carpenter v. Stephen F. Austin State University (706 F2d 6708 [1983]).
7. Brito v. Zia Company (478 F2d 1200 [1973]).
8. Ramirez v. Hofheinz (619 F2d 442 [1980]).
9. Zell v. United States (472 F.Supp. 356 [1979]).
10. Rowe v. General Motors (457 F2d 348 [1972]).
11. Harper v. Mayor and City Council of Baltimore (359 F.Supp. 1187 [1972]).
12. Marquez v. Omaha District Sales Office, Ford Division of the Ford Motor Company (440 F2d 1157 [1971]).
13. Turner v. State Highway Commission of Missouri (31 EPD 33, 352 [1982]).

PART 2

Approaches to Performance Evaluation

Performance and Productivity

————————— O. Glenn Stahl

No organized enterprise can escape making judgments about the be-havior and effectiveness of its staff. Assignment, advancement, re-ward, utilization, motivation, and discipline—all depend on such judgments, whether they are formalized and recorded or whether they are simply implicit in the actions of management. Yet, efforts to be systematic about evaluation of employee performance are fraught with uncertainty and disenchantment. Despite periodic surges of enthusiasm and a formidable literature on the subject, it remains an almost intractable problem, which has engendered fre-quent disillusionment.

Perhaps this condition should not be too disturbing. There is an understandable tension in our society between a philosophy of com-petitive performance and one of equalitarianism. Almost instinc-tively we appreciate the necessity for recognizing achievement and distinguishing it from mediocrity if we are to continue to thrive as a people; yet we shrink from making judgments about our fellow citi-zens and workers that may be invidious. This perpetual tension is evident in our approach to performance appraisal in the work place. Instead of permitting this to inhibit us, we should accept the chal-lenge to find modes of reconciliation between the need to evaluate and the desire to protect—even if these modes must be rediscovered in each generation. In effect, this is what the study of performance evaluation is really all about—a continual process of reconciling the necessity for productive organizations to make distinctions among people with the compulsion to ensure equity in human relation-ships.

The basic difficulties we must accept in the evaluation process are twofold: (1) finding the ways to appraise and report performance that are meaningful and useful in their impact upon the work to be done and (2) finding the ways to carry on the process and apply its results in full recognition that the process itself is a prime factor affecting employee motivation and morale. The second one is the principal object of debate, inquiry, and soul-searching. Most managers (and employees, for that matter) would probably agree that evaluation should (1) maintain or improve performance, not retard it; (2) support supervisory responsibility for the ultimate effectiveness of the work performed; and (3) assure reasonable equity and dignity in human relationships. This is no small order. About all a rational treatment of the subject can attempt is to draw upon what is known from experience and modest research and to season this knowledge with a generous quantum of intuition, insight, and speculation.

Objectives

Before we distill the more specific problems and venture some of their solutions, it is well that we think first in terms of objectives. Experience suggests that appraising and reporting on people's performance should serve these ends:

1. *Clarification of what is expected*—that is, to develop
    standards of satisfactory performance, setting forth what
    quality and quantity of work of a given type is acceptable and
    adequate for pursuing the functions of the organization.
2. *Fortifying and improving employee performance*—by
    identifying strong and weak points in individual achievement,
    recording these as objectively as possible, and providing
    constructive counsel to each worker.
3. *Refinement and validation of personnel techniques*—serving as
    a check on qualification requirements, examinations,
    placement techniques, training needs, or instances of
    maladjustment.
4. *Establishment of an objective base for personnel actions*—
    namely, in selection for placement and promotion, in
    awarding salary advancements within a given level, in
    making other awards, in determining the order of retention
    at times of staff reduction, and in otherwise recognizing
    superior or inferior service.

The traditional method for serving these purposes has been to require every supervisor and manager at fixed intervals (such as a year) to follow certain prescribed criteria, to render a judgment about how each subordinate measures up to these, to record these conclusions on a "rating" report of some kind, to discuss the results with the employee being appraised, and to submit the reports to his superior officer for review, after which they were to be deposited at some central point for future reference. Problems have been encountered in almost every effort to follow this general pattern.[1]

Common problems

Objectifying standards   Evaluation implies relating the work or behavior of an individual against some standard or norm concerning factors believed to be significant in the work. This is a point of key tie-in with efforts at improving productivity; where the work standards are not realistic and clear, hopes for good productivity cannot be high.

The standard may be subjective (as in the case of the quality of a piece of administrative writing) or objective (as in the case of the number of audit vouchers accurately processed), but it is an inescapable first step in any rational appraisal system. The aim is to make the standard as objective and consistent as possible. Otherwise evaluations will be of low reliability, with the criterion varying from one supervisor to another or varying in application to different employees by the same supervisor. Achieving objectivity has been one of the most frustrating aspects of performance appraisal. One of the principal solutions has been to enlist deep employee involvement in establishing the work criteria, a subject to which we shall return later.

Determining what to appraise   The employee's performance, not himself, should be the subject of analysis. In spite of the common-sense appearance of this statement, the fact is that traditional rating systems focused the supervisor's attention upon personal traits and characteristics of people rather than upon the actuality of what they did. Thus, emphasis was placed upon items such as tact, initiative, integrity, ingenuity, dependability, and the like. The alternative, and the one more commonly stressed nowadays, is to require evaluation of actual and concrete achievements or behavior on the job, without trying to translate this into a picture of the employee's personality. This approach is, of course, consistent with the concept of management by objectives wherein evaluation is concentrated upon the results, not just upon technique. The supervisor, who sees only a segment of the employee's life and behavior, is less likely to appreciate the person's generic traits than he is to gauge what emerges from the employee's mind or hands as a work product. Hence, the reporting system that is likely to evoke the most reliable findings is one that asks supervisors to cite and measure specific instances of performance in terms of the job demands.[2]

There are, to be sure, some difficulties with trying to report actual performance and specific behavior. Most important, it requires that rating forms be geared to each general category of work, so that the reporting official can be prompted to take note of each significant element of performance. The same form could not be used for police officers, stenographers, teachers, and nurses. Each occupation calls for quite different kinds of tasks, and there are vastly different criteria for and ways of observing their accomplishment. Perhaps the only things common to all jobs are the basic human personality traits of the type referred to previously, which explains why early rating systems tended to concentrate upon them. But the extra work called for in developing specialized appraisal forms for at least broad categories of occupations is completely justified on the grounds that evaluation must, if it is not to run afoul of many other pitfalls, focus upon the realities of the employee's work, upon the quality and quantity of his output, whether it is a service or a product. Specialized forms are the only means so far devised to facilitate this emphasis.

Another problem is that of ensuring that the performance or on-the-job behavior reported is representative and not exceptional. It is very easy to recall the exceptional and to overlook the normal. About the only solution to this problem is to maintain a constant campaign, through written instructions and training, alerting supervisors to the danger. The design of the report form itself may also help to remind evaluators of the need to look at performance in total perspective.

Relying upon questionable assumptions   Experience indicates that faith is misplaced in the following elements:

1. *A single tool*   In both industry and government a fundamental error has been to attempt to achieve all ends with a single evaluation device. The typical annual performance rating, which is expected to be usable for future promotion competition, for diagnosing training needs, for salary advancement, and for order of layoff, and in addition to serve as a stimulus to better performance and represent an honest and valid appraisal, has understandably been found wanting. No known method of ordering judgments or recording them has been able to satisfy such diverse purposes all at the same time. Consequently, current thinking has been directed toward the use of special methods, each tailored to suit a particular purpose.[3] For example, in the matter of promotion it has been concluded by many that selection for unknown future vacancies—with their variety of special qualification requirements—cannot be geared to previously recorded appraisals of past performance. Thus, the solution has been to seek further evaluations aimed directly at promotability of employees, as distinct from past performance per se, or to rely upon ad hoc appraisals at the time candidates are actually under

consideration for a specific vacancy, rather than to store up ratings for future reference without knowing the precise use likely to be made of them.

2. Fixed periods   Requiring supervisors annually or at some other fixed period to render a written evaluation on each employee has been another bane of modern rating systems. Supervisors are reluctant to go over old ground with long-term employees especially, and they often recoil from the artificiality of a process that seems to say: "Today I consider how my employees are doing," as if all the rest of the time does not count. Many do not hesitate to deal forthrightly with their subordinates on their daily work products or behavior, giving counsel on what is wrong and what might improve the situation as each occasion requires, but shrink from an effort to sum this all up and confront each employee with a periodic accounting of his total performance. In fact, some feel that this forced confrontation is at best awkward, replete with possibilities of each party saying the wrong thing, and at worst disruptive of what may otherwise be a salutary relationship.

Consequently, various ways to circumvent the dilemma between the genuine need for some kind of reporting and the problem of fixed periods have been devised. One has been to eliminate frequent ratings for long-term employees and require an appraisal on them only once every five years, or whenever they change jobs, and then only to verify if there has been any marked change in conduct or production. Another is to gear performance reports to specific events instead of to the calendar, so that they are made only when new supervisors have taken over, when employees are new to the job, when reorganizations have taken place, when the job content or technology has been changed, or on similar occasions. Still another variant is to confine regular reporting only to exceptional performance, either unusually superior or unusually poor, so that no reports at all need to be made on the great majority of workers in any given category. Under this last condition the appraisal and whatever motivational influence it might have are left to the day-to-day supervisor-employee relationship.[4]

3. Overall evaluations   Another implicit error has been to assume that we can analyze all of the faults and strengths of an employee, add them up in some fashion, and come to some neat overall conclusion—expressed by an adjective, a percentage or numerical value, a letter category, or some other device—that makes it possible to compare him as a whole with someone else. This is a most doubtful, if not actually a dangerous, procedure. Individuals on similar work may differ from each other in such a way that the strengths of one are in the very areas in which the other is weak. One employee may be good at meeting and dealing with people but not so good in expressing himself in writing; the other may be just the opposite, facile at paper-and-pencil articulation but shy and dull when it comes to face-to-face communication. If the job requires both skills in some measure, who is to say which employee is the better of the two? Together, with a deft organization of the work, they may make a pretty good team, even though individually they have shortcomings. Looking at the situation as a whole, no one can say that the total effect is not contributory to getting a good job done.

One solution to this problem of overall rating is to abandon the summation or conclusion but keep the analytical part of the report. Thus, a report might point up certain areas of activity or aptitude in which the individual excels and others in which he needs improvement but refrain from facilely labeling the total person into some grand category derived from these elements, especially if the latter is used as a means for comparison with others. An employee is usually able to recognize and accept his shortcomings in very specific aspects of his work but finds invidious and ego-shattering any attempt to pin a descriptive label on his total worth. Without such summary ratings it is doubtful that there would be as many challenges to supervisory judgments in the form of appeals against appraisals. Employees are not so likely to object to the "profile" of their behavior but may well resent any oversimplified conclusions drawn from it. They may feel, and sometimes rightly so, that what they excel in offsets what they do poorly. In any event, an analytical profile of performance can be even more useful in future applications than the summary evaluation, since the latter with its usual "halo" effect may detract attention from the concrete performance elements that are really important.

Impact of appraisals   As noted earlier, one of the most important considerations in performance evaluation is the impact the process itself has upon employee attitudes and performance. It took many years of experience before this factor was recognized and expressed, and only in the decade of the 1960s did research begin modestly to penetrate this facet of the subject. We have learned, for example, that sometimes the process of appraisal, particularly when it is a repetitive one with little relevance to the needs of the moment, inhibits good performance rather than insures it. This is especially true when there have been flaws in the employee's performance and these are brought to his attention in an inept fashion. Nor does it follow that a periodic reminder to an employee as to how good he is necessarily serves to maintain his level of accomplishment. It may even motivate him to slacken up a little because of overconfidence.

There is no question that, by and large, employees need to "know where they stand" in the eyes of their superiors. The error comes in assuming that this truism is universal and invariable. For example, take the case of an employee whose weaknesses are tolerable though nonetheless real. He meets minimum standards, perhaps by extra effort or other offsetting characteristics, so that management is not prepared to do anything very drastic about his shortcomings. It decides that the deficiencies are more or less irreparable and that the organization would best live with them, make any necessary adjustments, and adapt the employee's positive talents in some direction that minimizes the effects of the weaknesses. In the face of this bit of reality, traditional rating philosophy would ordain that management, once a year or during some other interval, bring up to the employee what these weaknesses are. The chances are that these repeated reminders would only serve to develop him into a thoroughly unsatisfactory employee. The persistent laying-it-on-the-line theme would tear down his ego to the point where he loses all self-respect.

In short, periodic reminders are not likely to be very productive of the object of improving performance unless they introduce something new to the situation or unless the time has come to jolt an employee into a new pattern of behavior. They may even be counterproductive. Employee performance—to say nothing of the subtleties of the ongoing supervisor-employee relationship—is a delicate and sensitive matter. Wholesale handling of infinite varieties of situations without regard to human differences and the sundry emotional needs of employees is almost certain to precipitate anything from disappointment to disaster.

Gauging potential   A common pitfall is the failure to look beyond past performance as a predictor for the future. So much attention has been focused on past performance that measures of a person's potential not demonstrated on his existing job have been underplayed. Too often aptitudes or skills actually possessed by a person but not brought into evidence in past positions are overlooked.

It is for this reason that aptitude tests supplementary to performance records are often used in promotion selection. This is a sound procedure, provided the abilities tested are genuinely needed in the post being filled. The best example is when selections must be made from among nonsupervisory employees to fill supervisory jobs. In personnel matters the past is not always prologue, at least not completely so. A serious mistake is made by organizations that base promotions to *new jobs* entirely upon performance in quite *different jobs* or, worse still, upon simple seniority.

Another means to get at employee potential has been to ask supervisors to appraise this factor separately from performance.[5] Such a process obviously must be quite subjective, since it rests entirely upon a general sizing up of a person by a superior official who may or may not be good at this kind of exercise. A tangential issue is whether or not the employee should be entitled to know what his supervisor thinks of his future. Even though there is almost general accord on the practice of allowing employees to know the details of the appraisals of their past performance, management tends to shrink from revealing so intangible a prediction as that represented by appraisal of potential. Clearly it is fraught with all kinds of dangers of misjudgment or prejudicial behavior by supervisors, but these flaws can be minimized by making certain that action based upon "potential" ratings is taken only when they are made by several different officers who have some acquaintance with the employee involved. Furthermore, they merely represent formalization of predictive judgments that are going to be made anyway at one point or another.

Disclosure   An issue of some consequence to employees, and one often exploited by their union representatives, is the matter of access to the results of the rating process. Of course, with a participative approach in which the rater and ratee are partners, the problem does not arise. But there was a time when ratings were considered so confidential that they were kept locked up in the office safe. Needless to say, such a procedure did not contemplate their use as instruments for positive improvement of performance. Even today final recordings are viewed by some managers as reports for the eyes of management only. It is highly doubtful whether a cooperative spirit can be sustained very long where employees are not allowed to see what the record says about their past performance.

A more complex problem arises when we refer to appraisals of potential. As may be inferred from the comments above, the highly subjective predictions implicit in supervisory descriptions of potential are purely opinion, can therefore be used only in combination with other devices that shape an employee's future, and would dry up into meaningless drivel if they had to be revealed (and therefore, in a sense, "justified") to employees. If management makes *adequate use of the techniques of multiple judgment*, both in potential appraisal itself and in the promotion process, there should be ample assurance to the employee that an offhand view of his prospects by some one individual will not be controlling in determining his future.

Employee participation in evaluation

Evaluation methods are worthless unless they have the full understanding, participation, and acceptance of the employees being appraised. In fact, the most progressive thinking on the subject concludes that supervisor and employee should *share* in the evaluation process, from start to finish.

A participative approach begins with the setting of work standards themselves, that is, the goals or norms by which success is to be judged. Where numerous workers are engaged in comparable tasks, this can be accomplished by a group effort in which the supervisor is leader and convenor but in which a serious attempt is made to arrive at a group consensus on standards of quality and quantity that are in the interests of the organization as a whole but are also within the bounds of reasonableness so far as human realization is concerned. A similar process can be pursued with one-of-a-kind workers on an individual basis. Experience has demonstrated that standards of performance that employees have helped shape are the most durable, the most valid, and the most operable.

In addition, there must be participation in the evaluation itself. With due allowance for the reservations about periodicity already stated, the wise supervisor begins his appraisal, not merely ends it, by consultation with the person being evaluated. Citing the standards that have been the product of a joint effort, he solicits as much self-analysis as possible from an employee and tries to make his final report a reflection of concurrence between the two parties. In aggravated cases this may not always be an attainable goal, but it is usually worth the try.

Not to lose sight of some of the points made in foregoing paragraphs, it should be understood, of course, that the participative process is most successful when it is used at a point of need that is obvious to both supervisor and employee alike, not merely to meet some thoughtless requirement for annual review, which in some cases at least, may mean plowing old ground over and over again. Also, emphasis should always be upon the constructive side, that is, upon improvement, not just evaluation for evaluation's sake. And it should be recognized that workers improve most when specific goals are set and when the behavior of the supervisor during an appraisal session is consistent with his usual style and behavior on the job.

Methods of evaluation in use

A cursory review of what public jurisdictions are doing by way of performance appraisal is not encouraging, although a few places are exemplary in both their willingness to experiment and their capitalizing on what employers have learned about the process. Under the Civil Service Reform Act of 1978, the U.S. government has embarked upon a highly decentralized system wherein each department develops and operates its own evaluation plans in accordance with very general guidelines. The broad directives issued by the Office of Personnel Management seem constructive, but it will be some time before their impact can be assessed.[6] A survey of 50 cities and 39 states, however, reveals a preponderance of the old standard devices of annual, numerically expressed, overall ratings, although the results are discussed with employees in 90 percent of the jurisdictions and they ostensibly have some influence on salary adjustments and promotions. Small consolation though it may be, the same study showed practice in private business not to be much more innovative except for greater use of essay-type performance reports.[7]

Perhaps the main hope in the governmental sector will stem from the amount of experimentation that will be stimulated by the new federal program and by expectation that state and local governments will continue their diversity of practice—one of the old bulwarks of a federal system of government. The remainder of this article will be devoted to a brief summary of the major kinds of evaluation systems now in use, a discussion of who should do the appraising and a few words on administration.

Forms of reporting   Beginning with the U.S. Army's World War I "man-to-man comparison" scale, with its emphasis upon traits instead of tasks, and ranging up to highly complex schedules in mid-century, which sought to translate performance into numerical values, with little focus on the supervisor-employee relationship, many a rating system once in vogue has all but disappeared. The long-standing aim throughout the years had been to minimize personal bias that might enter into the process. But efforts to obviate bias by elaborate schedules and automatic scoring led mostly to disappointment and mystification of all parties involved.[8] The more common methods that are current are these:

1. Production records   These are more likely used as *parts* of reporting or *supplementary* to other methods. They are limited to work that lends itself to measurement of actual units of production, such as machine operators, voucher auditors, claims examiners, and the like. Where they take quality of work product into account, where they are supplemented by appraisal of employee behavior in relation to fellow workers and clients (often as important as raw production), and where standards for measurement result from employee-supervisor cooperation, production counts can be very useful and certainly have the advantage of being objective.

2. Graphic rating scales   These consist of a list of actions relating to job success and various descriptive phrases denoting degrees to which the employee's performance is reflected in each of these items. Usually presented along a horizontal line for each action item or factor, graphically portraying the range of quality (hence the name), these degrees of performance serve as a guide to the supervisor, who must mark the phrase most aptly describing the employee's behavior or performance on each factor.

Graphic scales are most dependable when the descriptive phrases at each gradation along a factor-scale have been sharpened by preclearance with many supervisors, who choose which phrases best represent different values, and/or when performance factors and examples of high, medium, and low performance ("anchors") have been identified by employees to whom they will apply (behaviorally anchored scales). In these cases, successive groups review the factors and anchors, and when it comes to ultimate application, final ratings are made by two supervisors in each case. Without such safeguards, scales that rely upon mere arbitrary weights or values given to each gradation create an appearance of precision, lending a stamp of scientific legitimacy to what are simply subjective judgments of the rating-form designers. In any event, if gradations on each item relate to realistic norms, if the factors cover actual job behavior rather than inferred personal traits, and if there is no adding up of item scores in the form of a spurious "conclusion" rating, a graphic device can facilitate supervisor-employee joint discussion, and each individual item may have more validity standing alone than when all are aggregated.

3. Critical incident method   This calls for a recording *from time to time* of actual critical incidents in the employee's work that illustrate either good or poor performance, based upon the usual determination of major performance requirements and thus varying with different occupations. The resulting work sheet becomes a realistic record of some concrete experiences; it serves as a profile of the employee's pattern of behavior, bringing out both effective and ineffective incidents. It can be useful in facilitating employee consultation, and it has the virtue of focusing on facts. However, it does run the risk of overemphasis on unusual behavior, because it leads the supervisor into looking for those incidents that typify the especially good or bad, to the possible neglect of performance that is average but even more typical of the individual's total behavior.

4. Narrative reports   These are simply free-written formats, sometimes structured by use of outlines or guides to ensure completeness and care but in other cases allowing the supervisor to express himself as he sees fit on aspects of performance he chooses to cover. Assuming that no summary rating or conclusion about the "whole person" is attempted, narrative reports—which are really among the oldest forms of evaluation ever employed—make possible maintenance of records on performance that might otherwise be lost or forgotten but without the flaws of more formal or scaled devices. Furthermore, they permit flat statements of fact, to which employees are not as likely to take exception as they are to moralizing categorizations of their performance. Free-written reports do not lend themselves to ready comparative treatment, but the doubts about such a use of evaluations are sufficient to make this shortcoming less important. They can be most effective in future placement and in developing mutual understanding between supervisor and subordinate.

5. Coaching appraisal   This involves a continuous joint exploration between supervisor and employee as to how the latter is getting along, thus emphasizing a relationship rather than a format or device. Whatever props may be used to help structure the discussions, they are not confined to specified periods, and they aim primarily at fostering mutual understanding and improving performance. Thus, this approach becomes more a mode of supervision than simply a rating method.

Variations as to who evaluates   Aside from the prevalent method of rating employees by their individual supervisor, other means of getting at the appraisals have been tried, among them:

1. Multiple or group appraisal   This involves evaluation of an individual's work by several persons at the same time and has been used by government agencies and business establishments primarily for upper-level supervisors and executives. It usually consists of appraisal of the manager's performance and potential by a panel of superiors acquainted with his work from different vantage points, including his line supervisor; review of the group's conclusions by the next higher level of management authority to relate them to overall organization effectiveness, possible reassignments, and the like; discussion by the superior with the subject individual, pointing out strengths and weaknesses and suggesting action growing out of the group appraisal and review; and guiding development of the person through further training, greater delegation of authority, rotational assignment, committee work, and comparable steps. Variations on the technique include, for example, the possibility of permitting the subject executive to choose one of the members of the panel that will make the group appraisal in his case. The process, having arisen from concern with executive development, illustrates the advantage of special-purpose evaluation over the omnibus methods that have encountered so many difficulties and raised so many doubts. It is an expensive process but undoubtedly worth the cost when dealing with key employees.

2. Self-appraisal   This is simply evaluation by each employee of his own progress, subject to review. Most experiments have shown that employees tend to be more severe in estimating their performance value and sizing up where they need to improve than are their supervisors. Whether there is a formal means for employee self-appraisal or not, certainly it is profitable for the supervisor to take the subject of the evaluation in on the process and to help him and lead him, if necessary, into an appraisal in which he recognizes his own faults and virtues. This is likely to make the process a mutually acceptable one and relieves the supervisor of making the judgment alone. The problem of performance evaluation and recording becomes a joint enterprise, as much the responsibility of the employee as it is of his chief. As in so many aspects of this subject, however, room must be left for determination of those instances where the technique may be useful and where it may not.

3. *Appraisal by peers and subordinates*   This entails evaluation of each member of a work unit by all the others, by colleagues and subordinates as well as by supervisors. Sometimes referred to as "mutual rating," it is the most unusual and least-used of the modern approaches. A collective result, reflecting the interaction of judgments of peers and subordinates in addition to superiors, may develop a balanced and interesting profile of the employee's behavior on the job. While not guaranteeing objectivity, it certainly helps preclude bias. Although it may not produce neat summaries about people that permit comparison with others, the method has all the advantages of wide participation and can serve constructive guidance and counseling purposes. At least it deserves more research attention than it has so far received.

Administration of appraisal systems

A few precepts regarding the operation of an evaluation system, however formalized or informal it happens to be, may be safely enunciated. For one thing, it is imperative that any formal procedure be simple, expeditious, and not unduly burdensome on supervisors. Processes and forms that demand hours of study and consultation on each case at specific points in time invariably break down. Even where formal recording is expected only for extraordinary performance, it is wise to keep the load on already busy supervisors at a minimum so as not to encourage ignoring the exceptional performance that should be reported.

Of equal merit is the need for continuous training of rating officials in the objectives and processes of evaluation that are used in the organization. Many difficulties can be reduced, if not eliminated, by adequate attention to a sophisticated program of clarification. Frank acknowledgment of its limitations and pitfalls, full participation of managers at all levels in development, and critical audit of the system will go far to elicit the understanding and cooperation of the operating branches. Training and participation are really parts of the same concept. The one must be achieved largely through the other, and they may be pursued through planned conferences that serve both purposes.

Any plan leading to written reports should provide for systematic review of lower-level determinations by higher echelons in the hierarchy. Where managers above the first rating level have some contact and acquaintance with an employee's work, they should be participants at some point in the evaluation. Likewise, this is the point where unevenness in the practices or judgments of various supervisors may be brought into closer harmony. It is only here that the overly permissive supervisor and the unusually rigid or austere one can have their deviations from the norm made clear to them and their attitudes and appraisal practices brought into more acceptable balance.

Many students of the subject in recent years have concluded that performance reports, if they are to facilitate good performance, should not be primary instruments of discipline. Wherever performance is so wanting that there is no alternative to a self-respecting manager but to dismiss or demote an employee, this should be done forthwith at the time when conditions call for it, not as the result of "discovering" the circumstances on the occasion of a performance review. The latter should be reserved for the explicit purpose of joint analysis between supervisor and subordinate as to where the work stands, a taking stock of how things are going and how each of them can contribute to more effective achievement. It need be no more threatening or punitive than inventorying materials and supplies—more difficult and requiring more care, yes, but not more offensive. Punishment for poor work should not wait for formal "rating time." Under pressure to demonstrate sensitivity to productivity improvement, some jurisdictions—including the federal service—seem bent upon ignoring such reasoning.

Another important point relates to professional workers. Evaluation of their performance may be crucial to an enterprise's viability and success. Systems fitting the masses of employees are seldom suitable for professionals. The importance of their status with their peers, both inside and outside the organization, must be taken into account. And, as we shall see later, recognition of their achievements by outside groups must be carefully cultivated and coordinated with inside recognition.

The matter of administration should not be closed without another reference to participation. To encourage sound and useful appraisal, management should be mindful that both in the design of the system and in its operation there should be ample opportunity built in for all interested parties—supervisors, managers, and employees—to participate in the total process. In those instances where formal ratings have some effect upon personnel actions, provision should also be made for any employee rated adversely to appeal the judgment rendered to some impartial hearing officer or committee empowered to advise top management on final disposition, just as if it were any other kind of grievance.

1. Useful references on appraisals, including analyses of many different solutions to problems, are: Felix M. Lopez, Jr., *Evaluating Employee Performance*, Washington, D.C., International Personnel Management Association, 1968 (the most comprehensive treatment); two pamphlets by the U.S. Office of Personnel Management, Washington, D.C.: *Employee Performance Evaluation, A Practical Guide to Development and Implementation for State, County, and Municipal Governments*, November 1979 and *A Guide for Improving Performance Appraisal, A Handbook* (by Priscilla Levinson), 1980; and Kenneth J. Lacho, G. Kent Stearns, and Maurice F. Villere, "A Study of Employee Appraisal Systems of Major Cities in the United States," *Public Personnel Management*, March–April 1979, pp. 111–125.

2. This approach is in less danger of deserving the trenchant criticism of work evaluations made by Douglas McGregor in "An Uneasy Look at Performance Appraisal," *Harvard Business Review*, May–June 1957, pp. 89–94. In this classic article McGregor accused supervisors of "playing God" when they seek to judge the whole person.

3. One piece of evidence discrediting all-purpose ratings was the research conducted in the General Electric Company as reported in Herbert H. Meyer, Emanuel Kay, and John R. P. French, Jr., "Split Roles in Performance Appraisal," *Harvard Business Review*, January–February 1965, pp. 123–129.

4. As long ago as the reports of the two Hoover Commissions on the federal civil service (1949 and 1955), there was a lack of support for regular periodic ratings. The first commission urged that "ability and service records" be used only for the supervisor-employee conference, with a view to developing employee performance, and not to govern salary increases, layoffs, or dismissals (Commission on Organization of the Executive Branch of the Government, *Personnel Management: A Report to the Congress*, Washington, D.C., February 1949, p. 33). The Second Hoover Commission followed this up with the recommendation that only exceptional performance—the kind demonstrating promotion potential, misplacement, or need for special recognition or dismissal—be reported. It advised that a rating system "should not be an end in itself" (Commission on Organization of the Executive Branch of the Government, *Personnel and Civil Service*, Washington, D.C., February 1955, pp. 62–65).

5. A number of U.S. federal agencies, including the Foreign Service, have tried this approach, usually with moderate success.

6. See, for example, the 1980 Guide, op. cit.

7. Lacho, Stearns, and Villere, loc. cit.

8. Reference to earlier editions of this text will demonstrate the evolution of these systems.

Positive Program for Performance Appraisal

Alva F. Kindall and James Gatza

"Bill, it's time for your annual appraisal interview. You've done a lot of good work, and I want you to know that it has been noticed and appreciated. Of course there are areas in which improvements can be made. Let's start with the good side. Your output record has been good all year, and we're particularly pleased with your showing on the cost control project. You have good judgment, and it shows up in your planning. As I told you at the time, you did a swell job on the Clarkson order. . . .

"Now, Bill, let me tell you where I think you can make some improvement. I know that I can speak frankly and come right to the point. Your stubbornness is still a major problem. I can think of two or three times I had to step in to settle a dispute between you and the boys in central planning. I'm sure you agree that you haven't shown much imagination or creativity in doing your job, and this is an area the company thinks is important, especially when picking people for higher management jobs. Another thing I've noticed, Bill, is that you've been too aggressive in your dealings with other departments. You know, we all have to pull together if this company. . . ."

What's going on here? In our opinion, *quackery*! You recognize the "conversation" above as the interview associated with a performance appraisal program. Formalized appraisal programs are widely used today, under a variety of names, for promotion, demotion, transfer, retention, retirement, executive development, spotting training needs, evaluating psychological tests, and other organizational purposes. Many of these programs fail to meet their objectives and often do real damage. Why do they fail? Why do they induce quackery? And in particular, what kind of performance appraisal *is* more effective? What exactly would the managers of a company do—what specific steps would they follow—to adopt a program that would help employees take greater responsibility and contribute more fully to the goals of the organization? These are the questions we shall discuss in this article.

Why typical programs fail

Many businessmen are personally familiar with the shortcomings of conventional appraisal programs. The topic has also been a favorite one of writers.[1] The most important reasons for failure can be summarized as follows:

As the illustration at the beginning of this article suggests, the appraisal procedure leads the superior to judge his subordinate in terms of his personality traits. Some of the more popular traits mentioned in company rating forms are: mental alertness, integrity, initiative, adaptability, common sense, job interest, and self-confidence.

Now, it is one thing for an executive to react to another person's personality when "sizing him up." We do that every day. But it is quite another thing for a manager to delve into the personality of a subordinate in an official appraisal that goes into the records and affects his career. The latter amounts to quackery—to a pretension to training or knowledge which is not in fact possessed. For only in rare instances is a business executive properly qualified to assess the personality of an individual and, more important, to try to get the individual to change aspects of his personality. The human personality is a complex and highly abstract concept. Even psychologists disagree on how it should be defined or approached. Personality traits are themselves extremely difficult to define. Where does one draw the line, for example, between intelligence and common sense, or between self-confidence and aggressiveness?

A useful way of looking at the organizational appraisal process is to note the difference between *causes* and *results* of a person's behavior. In our illustrative interview, the disputes mentioned between the appraisee, Bill, and the central planning department are the *results* of Bill's behavior—observable events that took place. But the contention that Bill is stubborn represents his superior's attempt to identify the *cause* of these disputes. Looking at it in terms of such a distinction raises questions such as these: How accurate is the word "stubborn" as a description of Bill's actions? Is the superior qualified to choose one or more trait names or adjectives which correctly portray Bill as a person? Do Bill and his superior agree on what is meant by stubbornness and how it is different from assertiveness, tenacity, and other traits? Does the very word stubbornness put Bill in a defensive attitude and block further communication?

If a superior raises an issue in terms of the results he has observed, the discussion tends to fasten upon the facts, their significance, and what they suggest in terms of future action. But communication is greatly hampered, we feel, when the superior presents the issues in terms of what *he feels* are the underlying cause factors involved. The subordinate may react defensively or argumentatively and block further communication to a large degree. This problem is, in our view, a major reason why a great many appraisal schemes have failed to accomplish what they are intended to do. "Improving performance" and "developing people" are two of the most common appraisal plan goals. It seems obvious that the appraisal process cannot go far toward attaining these goals unless there is effective communication between the evaluator and the person being evaluated.

Douglas McGregor makes a lasting addition to the managerial vocabulary when he likens the superior's role under many appraisal plans to that of "playing God." He states that the superior does not want to pass judgment upon another person when his judgment may have a great influence on that individual's future.[2] As a result, the superior resists the role of "playing God," and will avoid it in various ways. For instance, the superior may ignore a company rule that he discuss the rating with his subordinate. Another common occurrence reflecting this resistance is actually rather ludicrous: practically all of the managers in an organization will be rated "above average."

Practical objectives

So much for the inadequacy of common appraisal procedures. Let us turn now to the kind of approach that will work—that will encourage imagination, ingenuity, the acceptance of responsibility, and more intelligent efforts to achieve organizational goals.

Consider the following three points as a statement of objectives for organizational performance appraisal:

1. The first and focal objective is the improvement of performance in the job now held. This suggests that the appraisal procedure should not stop at an examination of the past; it should move on to the preparation of some plan for future action based on what has been learned from the past. This also suggests that the appraisal plan should embrace as many positions as possible, and that it should strive for improvement in all of them.
2. The second goal is the development of people in two senses: (*a*) providing the organization with people qualified to step

into higher positions as they open up; (*b*) serving as a help to the individual who wishes to acquire the knowledge and abilities he needs to become eligible for a higher job.

3. The appraisal procedure should also provide answers to the two questions which seem to be the recurrent concern of almost every organization member: "How am I doing?" and "Where do I go from here?" Answering these questions is of obvious benefit to the person whose mind they occupy. It may also be of great value to the organization, for in many cases these questions will preoccupy an individual and prevent him from hearing or responding to much of what his superior has to say.

This statement of objectives does not cover all possible goals, nor does it intend to. It makes no mention, for example, of two common appraisal program goals: providing an inventory of personnel resources, and providing a means for testing personnel procedures. There is, we feel, great danger in asking an appraisal program to do too many things at once. It tends to be more effective if the company has differentiated between its needs for appraising performance and its needs for a system of performance reporting.

Some organizations will need some kind of report on the qualifications or performance of its people. This is the case, for example, when the organization takes a personnel inventory at some point, or has need for a continuing manpower audit procedure. When this need is present, management should, we feel, devise a simple barebones report which carries only the information needed for these particular purposes. Our reasoning is this: All too often appraisal and reporting are looked on as one task. When this is done, the *performance report* usually is the same sheet of paper used as a guide in making the *appraisal*. The disadvantage of this practice is that it often leads the superior to sway his ratings out of conscious or unconscious concern over how the report might look to others.

Five-step program

The program we are about to discuss is not brand-new or original. A few companies have been using essentially similar programs for some time. Yet this approach is a new look in performance appraisal, standing in sharp contrast to the bulk of current appraisal practices. This plan is appropriate for the appraisal of executive, supervisory, sales, staff, and similar positions. It is somewhat more difficult to use in the case of the highly routinized production-line type of jobs.

Here in capsule form, is the program:

Step 1: the individual discusses his job description with his superior and they agree on the content of his job and the relative importance of his major duties—the things he is paid to do and is accountable for.

Step 2: the individual establishes performance targets for each of his responsibilities for the forthcoming period.

Step 3: he meets with his superior to discuss his target program.

Step 4: checkpoints are established for the evaluation of his progress; ways of measuring progress are selected.

Step 5: the superior and subordinate meet at the end of the period to discuss the results of the subordinate's efforts to meet the targets he had previously established.

Let us now look at this program in greater detail. To begin with, it is assumed that company-wide and major division objectives have been established and communicated to subordinate levels. It is further assumed that these goals have been expressed as targets whenever possible. As we shall use the term, a target is a clearly defined goal to be attained by a stipulated date. Whenever possible, the statement of a target includes the standard of performance to be reached. Thus, "to increase sales" is insufficient as a target statement, while "to increase sales 10% by December 31" is a workable target. There will, of course, be targets that cannot be expressed in such definite terms—for example, improving relations with another organization.

Job content In Step 1, the individual's job description is discussed, and he and his superior agree on what is involved in each of the major areas of his job. There should be a full understanding and a common accord on how much importance is attached to the various aspects of the person's job.

Performance targets Step 2 takes a little more explaining. The individual draws up a program of performance targets for his job in the immediate period ahead. Six months is usually an appropriate time period. This list of targets embodies his plans in all of the major areas of his job. The targets he selects should be *challenging*; they should represent improvements over the results thus far achieved. At the same time, they should be *realistic*; they should be attainable within the period selected. Of utmost importance, the entire target program should be *manageable*.

Most of the targets the individual establishes will probably be directly related to his job duties and the needs of the organization as expressed in part through similar target programs set at higher levels. To illustrate, an industrial equipment salesman might set up these targets, among others:

1. To increase total sales 8% or more.
2. To add four or more new accounts.

3. To at least double sales of the new product.
4. To regain at least one of the three accounts lost during the past year.
5. To improve relations with the X Company (a large customer).

In addition to these job-oriented goals, the individual may, if he wishes, include in his program targets related to his own promotional aspirations. Continuing with the illustration of a salesman, let us assume that the salesman is fully experienced in his job and has begun working toward eventual promotion to a sales managership. He is encouraged, under this appraisal plan, to ask this question: "How does the sales manager's job differ from mine?" Suppose that one of the sales manager's duties is to construct expense budgets and that the salesman has had no experience in drawing up a sales office expense budget. The salesman can include in his program a target such as this: "to be able to prepare without help a sales office expense budget."

Inclusion of personally oriented targets such as the one just cited strengthens the role of this performance appraisal program as a means of developing people. In some respects training experiences vie for the person's time with his immediate job duties. So his target program should, we feel, grant explicit recognition to his self-development goals and bring them into some sort of balance with goals concerning his job responsibilities.

Discussion of plan   In Step 3, the individual and his superior meet to discuss the target plan he has drawn up. The subordinate sets the pace: the discussion centers around the plan he has formulated. Under normal circumstances, the superior should not overrule him. Exercising a veto power may douse the enthusiasm a person normally feels about having the chance to plan his own affairs. The superior should adopt the role of counselor or consultant. Hopefully, both will learn more about the problems they face if the boss relies on *discussion* rather than *orders* as the means of influencing his subordinate. However, during times of economic crisis, the superior may want to take a stronger hand if the subordinate sets unmanageable targets or chooses targets which fail to meet pressing organizational needs.

The key step in this entire appraisal program is this third step, the superior-subordinate conference over the subordinate's target schedule. It is perhaps better to call it "tricky" than to imply that it is overly simple. We feel that the process of setting one's own performance targets is highly valuable both as a training experience and as a source of personal motivation. These advantages may be lost if the superior goes to the extreme of handling the conference in such a way as to make the subordinate doubt that he really has been granted the freedom to establish his own goals. At the opposite extreme, the superior who does not voice his thoughts about the subordinate's targets may destroy the merit of this appraisal program as a means of directing human efforts toward organizational goals. It should not be difficult to stay in the proper middle ground between these extremes; and emphasizing the superior's role as a counselor will help in this respect.

Determining checkpoints   In Step 4, the subordinate and his superior select checkpoints for the targets established. Checkpoints are merely appropriate points at which progress can be evaluated. The end of the appraisal period is not necessarily the best time at which to assess progress toward some of the targets selected. Many checkpoints will be found in the company's regular procedures for reporting output, sales, costs, profits, quality, and the like. A project completion date is an obviously suitable checkpoint. It will be necessary to create checkpoints for some target projects without clear ending or division times. This whole process may be highly rewarding as a source of greater understanding of company problems.

Closely connected with the selection of checkpoints is the designation of means of measuring progress. Questions such as these demonstrate the desirability of stating in advance what measures are to be used in appraising progress toward each target:

1.   Should a salesman's efforts be measured in terms of gross sales or sales net of returns?
2.   Is total cost or per-unit cost the more suitable measure of a department head's cost-reduction efforts?
3.   On the less tangible side, what things should be looked at when trying to evaluate progress toward a target of improved grievance handling?
4.   Going further, how should these various factors be combined in making the final evaluation?

It need hardly be said that means of measurement will seldom be perfect. Hopefully, this phase of the appraisal program will lead participants to devise better ways of evaluating organizational phenomena. In any event, we feel it necessary and valuable to have explicit discussion between superior and subordinate of the measurement problems involved in the targets which they have agreed upon.

At this stage the subordinate should write down the targets, checkpoints, and means of measurement. We prefer that this be done informally, and dislike the use of a standard form. Instead, the subordinate should write down the performance target program as he sees it, and give a copy to his boss. The major purpose for writing things down is to aid memory when his performance is being analyzed late. Some organizations will want a copy to go to the officer in charge of training, who can use these target programs as a source of information on company-wide training needs and activities. This is all right but procedures should not be elaborated. There is a danger that overformalization of the paper work may lead to the situation of the tail wagging the dog.

Checking the results   At the end of the agreed upon time period, the superior and subordinate meet to discuss the operating and other results that the subordinate has obtained. This is Step 5 in our suggested program. Their conversation naturally centers around how well the subordinate has done in pursuing the targets he had previously set.

Here is a key point in the understanding of this appraisal program: *hitting the target is not the measure of success.* It is to be expected that some targets will be surpassed, some never even approached. The person who sets meager targets and always hits them is certainly of no greater value to the company than the person who sets unreachably high targets, falls short consistently, yet in doing so makes substantial improvements over his past work.

If one's "score" in hitting the bull's-eye is not the important thing, what is? Simply this: the results achieved by the *total process* of establishing targets, striving to attain them, and analyzing what intervenes between planned and actual performance. When a judgment must be made, the individual is evaluated on his ability to set targets as well as his ability to attain them.

In checking results, we feel the superior should do all he can to emphasize successes—to build on successful accomplishment. In the case of unsuccessful accomplishment, the superior should help the subordinate. This help takes many forms: coaching, training, work assignment, allowing the subordinate to substitute for the superior, and so on.

There is nothing in the recommended appraisal procedure which suggests that a superior should abdicate his managerial responsibility. Suppose that after coaching, training, and other help, a subordinate still fails to set and reach targets deemed realistic by his superior. At this point the boss should act, even though it might mean demotion, transfer, or release of the subordinate.

Taking action

It has been convenient to express these as separate steps, although in practice the boundaries tend to blur. Also, of course, this is a continuous process, and the five steps are repeated each period. In addition, there should be a recognition of long-term targets as well as the shorter term ones we have used as illustrations. The stress on checkpoints should help in the handling of long-range goals and should facilitate their division into a series of subtargets.

Advantages gained   This appraisal program can be criticized on the grounds that it takes too much time. True, it does take time—certainly more time than is required to put a few checkmarks on a standard rating sheet. But how is that time spent? The superior and the subordinate spend their time planning, organizing, directing, controlling, innovating, and motivating. Isn't this the management job? If someone claims the executive does not have the time to do this, we suggest that he is really saying that he has no time to manage and wants to drop back to the old "do" part of his job.

On the other hand, the proposed program has six positive advantages for top management to consider.

1.   *The subordinate knows in advance the basis on which he is going to be judged.*
2.   *The superior and subordinate both agree on what the subordinate's job really is.*

In many situations adoption of this appraisal program may give the superior a better understanding of the subordinate's problems than he has ever had before.

3.   *The program takes place within the superior-subordinate relationship and should strengthen this relationship.*

Note that this program does not ask the superior to "play God," to be an all-powerful judge. It asks instead that he be a counselor and that he talk over the facts with his subordinate before he comes to an appraisal of the subordinate's performance.

4.   *The program has a self-correcting characteristic which tends to help people set targets that are both challenging and reachable.*

To illustrate, consider the case of a person who consistently sets his targets too low. He tends to reach them and surpass them all, thereby drawing attention to the level at which they have been set. In addition to this, an experienced superior should detect a low aim when the subordinate first presents his targets for discussion. Likewise, the person with an unrealistically high aim will soon enough begin to wonder why he is falling short of most of his targets.

5.   *The program provides a method of spotting training needs.*

A superior can see where a person needs help. The individual can see where he can benefit from added knowledge or skill. The same is true on a departmental or company-wide basis. A personnel director or training director can examine a number of the target programs and get some idea of where training emphasis should be placed. This appraisal plan is certainly not the only source of this information; yet in many cases it may add new and valuable data for use in the training effort. It should help eliminate "training for training's sake," which we have had so much of in recent years.

It may help manager development in yet another way. As suggested earlier, a promotion-minded individual can ask to see the target program of a position he seeks and use the information to prepare himself for the job and enhance his candidacy. He can ask himself: (1) What types of things must the occupant of the next higher position do well? (2) Am I able to do these types of things well? (3) What must I do to learn the other parts of the job well?

6. *This appraisal approach treats as a total process a person's ability to see an organizational problem, devise ways of attacking it, translate his ideas into action, incorporate new information as it arises, and carry his plans through to results.*

Thus, it highlights a sort of "total managerial action" in contrast to things we customarily factor out as conceptual entities— such things as the planning function, leadership ability, or financial knowledge. We think that manager selection will often be improved by this emphasis on the whole managerial job. Further, we contend that *the best predictor of future success as a manager is past success in managerial duties.* This appraisal program asks the executive to look at the record of managerial success, not the manager's personality.

Making the transition

How does an organization move over to this kind of performance appraisal? There can be various ways, of course, but we think that two ways should be given particular consideration.

The first avenue is the familiar "start at the top." The president or other chief executive would be the first to use the program, and its adoption would then proceed down the successive levels of the company. This way of going about the task has the strong virtue of emphasizing the relationship of company-wide objectives to those set at subordinate levels. It also allows people to experience first as subordinates a technique they will later employ as superiors. In addition, adoption from the top down tends to minimize the problems that might arise because a manager employs a practice his superior does not understand or sanction.

A second general way to make the transition to this new appraisal program is to install it in one segment of the organization, e.g., a branch, plant, or department. This might allow some degree of learning through experience before the program is extended to other segments of the company. It also has the virtue of allowing comparisons between units under the new program and those not yet involved. A company having a number of roughly similar branches might learn a good deal from this "control group" method of adoption. On the other hand, it might not be easy to transmit what has been learned to other organizational units, particularly if there are great differences in the type of work handled.

Whichever of these two ways (or possibly some other way) is preferred, the question of timing warrants attention. It hardly appears desirable for all managers to set their targets simultaneously. This makes it nearly impossible for the targets set at higher levels to be properly reflected in the targets set at subordinate echelons.

Temptations to avoid

There are two *caveats* concerning the adoption of the appraisal program we have recommended:

(1) *Don't rush it!* Appraisal through the target-setting approach involves ways of handling people that may differ greatly from the way people have been treated up to now in a given organization. It means moving from the authoritarian assumptions that Douglas McGregor has labeled "Theory X" to the more dynamic assumptions of his "Theory Y" (see the accompanying box). For one thing, the subordinate is granted a stronger voice in mapping out the content of his job. Not only that, he is allowed to speak first; his target plans are the starting point in his discussions with his superior. The organization also grants a form of recognition to his personal promotional goals. In short, there are a number of ways in which people's thinking, as well as their actions, will have to change if they are to make effective use of the appraisal program we have put forward.

This argument suggests that: (*a*) adoption of the program should be announced well in advance of the time initial actions are to take place; (*b*) each person involved should have time to talk the new procedures over with his superiors, subordinates, and other associates; (*c*) everyone involved should be given time to think through his ideas about the relative importance of various parts of his job. It seems advisable that a series of meetings be planned to ensure that people have a chance to discuss the full implications of self-target-setting. In addition to this, the actual drafting of targets will take time, especially the first time an individual is involved.

(2) *Don't force it!* As suggested in the discussion of Theories X and Y, there may be clusters of assumptions held by people which underlie their behavior toward others and the way in which they handle organizational problems. This suggests that there may be some people who are so strongly committed to the authoritarian assumptions of Theory X that they cannot long tolerate a procedure oriented toward a Theory Y conception of human motivation. They will find some way to avoid the procedure, misinterpret it, or thwart it. We feel that no one should be forced to participate in target-setting appraisal as outlined above. Instead, time should be allowed

The much discussed "Theory X" and "Theory Y" are labels coined by Douglas McGregor in *The Human Side of Enterprise* (New York, McGraw-Hill Book Company, Inc., 1960). They describe contrasting sets of management assumptions in industry today.

Under "Theory X," management makes these assumptions about behavior:

1. The average human being has an inherent dislike of work and will avoid it if he can.
2. Therefore, most people must be coerced, controlled, directed, and threatened with punishment if management is to get them to put forth adequate effort toward the achievement of organizational objectives.
3. The average human prefers to be directed, wishes to avoid responsibility, has relatively little ambition, and wants security above all.

The assumptions of "Theory X" are giving way to the newer concepts of "Theory Y." Here it is assumed that:

1. The expenditure of physical and mental effort in work is as natural as play or rest.
2. External control and the threat of punishment are not the only means for bringing about effort toward organizational objectives. Man will exercise self-direction and self-control in the service of objectives to which he is committed.
3. Commitment to objectives is a function of rewards associated with their achievement.
4. The average human being learns, under proper conditions, not only to accept but to seek responsibility.
5. The capacity to exercise a relatively high degree of imagination, ingenuity, and creativity in the solution of organizational problems is widely, not narrowly, distributed in the population.
6. Under the conditions of modern industrial life, the intellectual potentialities of the average human being are only partially utilized.

for him to observe the results and judge the effectiveness of the approach where it has been installed. It would be logically inconsistent to force a person to adopt against his wishes a program built around the notion that a manager should have a strong voice in planning the conduct of his job.

We have perhaps been overemphatic in stressing the caveats "don't rush it" and "don't force it." Many companies may be ready today for the immediate and rapid adoption of target-setting appraisal. Our purpose has been to underscore the wisdom of cautiousness during the transition period. We feel that no superior should be asked to participate until he has accepted the value of granting the subordinate the right to establish his own work targets.

Conclusion

The appraisal program we have sketched should be viewed as a function of the entire organization. It is not a personnel department "specialty." Nevertheless, the personnel manager has a particular role to play during the adoption of this program. He can give his attention to the evaluation of its effectiveness. We have proposed this appraisal program as a rather general system suitable for adoption in many organizations. We offer it as a starting point, and urge that its value be studied in each particular setting. Modifications should be made based on experience in its use. It is in this area that we see the personnel manager as a major contributor.

Measuring the results of this appraisal program is no easy task. To supplement the direct, more or less subjective evaluation which will doubtless take place, management would do well to:

1. Study personnel data: turnover, demotions, promotions, and the availability of qualified candidates when filling positions.
2. Study trends in needs for executive development and training activities.
3. Compare operating results: costs, output, sales, profits, savings, and the like. Of course there are severe limitations to the use of such end-result data in evaluating just one of the many things that contribute to final operating results. Nonetheless they may shed some light in certain cases.

In all of these areas, the company should seek ways of comparing measurements against each other, such as before-and-after collations and comparisons of one unit against another.

Of course, such problems are common to almost all appraisal programs. The unique aspects of the approach we recommend are its philosophy and objectives. Most appraisal practices used in business mirror the authoritarian thinking of "Theory X." In many instances company appraisal plans lead a manager to play psychologist and to "play God." Numerous company appraisal plans fail to meet their objectives because the plans fail to meet their objectives because the people involved are not qualified to act as psychologists, and they do not want to "play God."

Knowing that it is easy to criticize and more difficult to suggest improvements, we have put forward a performance appraisal program quite unlike most programs in use today. This program is, we feel, more consistent with the assumptions of "Theory Y." More than that, we contend that adoption of an appraisal program patterned along these lines may provide many organizations with a means of moving toward the Theory Y view that people can and will make their fullest contribution to the organization under conditions of greater self-direction and self-control.

1. See, for instance, Harold Mayfield, "In Defense of Performance Appraisal," *HBR* March–April 1960, p. 81; Douglas McGregor, "An Uneasy Look at Performance Appraisal," *HBR* May–June 1957, p. 89; and Philip R. Kelly, "Reappraisal of Appraisals," *HBR* May–June 1958, p. 59.

2. Op. cit.

How to Construct a Successful Performance Appraisal System

Craig Eric Schneier,
Richard W. Beatty, and Lloyd S. Baird

Few would argue that the design and implementation of an effective performance appraisal (PA) system for an entire organization, a department, or a work unit is one of the most difficult tasks faced by managers and human resource development (HRD) professionals. Surveys consistently indicate user dissatisfaction and recurring, costly revisions. Expectations are so low that a "good" performance appraisal system is often viewed as one in which managers simply complete the forms, after considerable prodding, and forward them to the personnel department to be filed. In a "poor" performance appraisal system, the forms are seldom even completed!

The frustration (and loss of credibility and power) of those in HRD over performance appraisal is matched by that of the users. Managers required to complete the ratings often see performance appraisals as another time-consuming, personnel-paperwork requirement, having little utility in solving such "real" managerial problems as meeting deadlines, containing costs, improving productivity, or deciding whom to promote. Subordinates being rated often view the performance appraisal system as yet another indication of management's capricious decision-making, subjectivity, and prejudice. They see few rewards given to those receiving the highest ratings withheld from those rated as merely average. In fact, almost everyone receives high ratings! Finally, neither raters nor ratees use the performance appraisal system as a tool to provide feedback and improve performance.

In short, even if the performance appraisal forms are completed, do the results matter? Is the performance appraisal system

Reprinted with permission of the authors from the April 1986 issue of *Training & Development Journal.*

actually used to make managerial decisions or solve managers' problems? Is it used to manage performance?

The key to improving the effectiveness of performance appraisal systems is not to design another form or fine-tune an existing form, but to design a performance management (PM) system. Such a system not only enables managers to solve performance problems, but also enables HRD specialists and staff to provide a useful tool and a successful program.

Deciding what to appraise

Appraisal systems fail for a variety of reasons (see Figure 1). For all but the most elementary jobs, identifying appropriate appraisal criteria is difficult. We legitimately can evaluate an assembly-line worker on the number of units which meet quality control standards, or a typist on accuracy, and we can measure their performance with agreed-upon methods. But what about initiative, appearance, tact, or organization skills? Should they be included, and if so, how should they be measured? When considering professional or administrative positions, or any positions with a variety of tasks, unprogrammed work, and complex requirements, the measurement problem becomes acute. Even if we can determine what ought to be measured, we must still determine how well people must perform. That is, performance standards themselves must be set. Exactly how many errors is the typist allowed to make per page? Or, how effective at leading group discussions must the manager be? Answers can vary across raters, across units within a single organization, and over time.

Many appraisal systems stress "objective" measures. Typically, these end up as easily quantified indices or deadlines that may not capture the essence of the work. The aim of appraisal systems is not to quantify everything, but rather to avoid arbitrary, capricious, or biased measurements (see Figure 2). Between objective and arbitrary measures are many based on sound judgment, agreed upon by raters and ratees, illustrated and defined fully, and related to job success. Expecting all measures to be "objective" is unrealistic and often irrelevant. Appraisal requires judgment.

Managers need to make informed, accurate, data-based judgments—some may be quantifiable, some not—about performance. The role of HRD staff is to provide the tools to help managers make these judgments and to monitor accuracy, consistency, and defensibility. To take out of appraisal the legitimate roles of observer, measurer, and judge under a guise of objectivity dooms the system to failure.

Judgment problems

The second set of performance appraisal problems comes from the raters. No matter how conscientious and well-meaning a rater may

Figure 1. Performance appraisal (PA) system problems, symptoms, and potential cures.

The measuring problem: Deciding what to evaluate	The judgment problem: Appraising performance	The policy problem: Using the results of the appraisal	The organization problem: Recognizing how managers work and the organization culture
Symptoms:	**Symptoms:**	**Symptoms:**	**Symptoms:**
Ambiguity in roles and responsibilities of each job	Disagreement on ratings	Top management fails to reward managers who are excellent in staff assessment and development	Appraisal forms not completed
Job performance is difficult to quantify	Reviewing official changes ratings		Managers complain about time requirements
No clear statement of overall objectives of units or organization	Appeals, grievances, accusations of bias, discriminations	Marginal performers receive promotions or salary increases	System perceived to belong to designers, not users
Appraisal contains only numerical indices			Personnel/human resource specialists take "enforcer," not "advisor" role
			System revised frequently
Potential cures:	**Potential cures:**	**Potential cures:**	**Potential cures:**
Job analysis and credible position description	Observable, behaviorally based criteria	Top management actually uses PA itself	Implement PA using the performance management (PM) model
Outcomes for each job identified	Performance documented over time	Policies governing use of PA consistently applied	
Overall goals of units and of organization set	Rater training and practice	Performance-contingent reward system in operation	
Train managers to make documented judgments	Effective communication of performance expectations		

Figure 2.   Measuring performance.

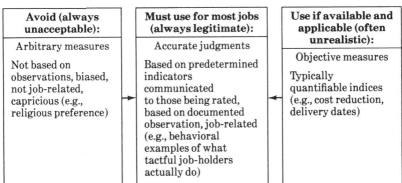

Avoid (always unacceptable):	Must use for most jobs (always legitimate):	Use if available and applicable (often unrealistic):
Arbitrary measures	Accurate judgments	Objective measures
Not based on observations, biased, not job-related, capricious (e.g., religious preference)	Based on predetermined indicators communicated to those being rated, based on documented observation, job-related (e.g., behavioral examples of what tactful job-holders actually do)	Typically quantifiable indices (e.g., cost reduction, delivery dates)

be, human judgment is subjective. We understand relatively little about observing behavior, recalling it, interpreting its causes and effects, evaluating its desirability, and ultimately rating an employee on an appraisal form. The manner in which the raters process information about a ratee's behavior may affect the results more than the ratee's behavior itself. Performance appraisal means judgment and information processing, not merely completing forms.

One manager might observe a subordinate performing well and attribute it to high ability. Another manager who views the same subordinate might feel the task was not very difficult. The first manager, attributing behavior to an internal cause (the subordinate's own ability) might give a high rating. The second manager, attributing behavior to an external cause (the nature of the task), might give a lower rating. People use their own conditioning, perspectives, values, expectations, philosophies, experiences, biases, prejudices, and interpersonal styles when making ratings. Due to judgment problems, performance appraisal becomes quite difficult, with lenient and otherwise less-than-accurate ratings common, regardless of the type of form used.

Few performance appraisal system users enjoy the prospect of setting standards. Managers can judge how well a person is doing in three ways (see Figure 3). People are successful in jobs because of what they achieve (results), what they do (behaviors), and/or what they are (personal characteristics).

Managers work with subordinates to determine what specific achievements, behaviors, and characteristics lead to successful performance and, with the assistance of HRD staff and the performer, develop viable standards. While there are innumerable varieties of

Figure 3.   Simplifying appraisal judgments.

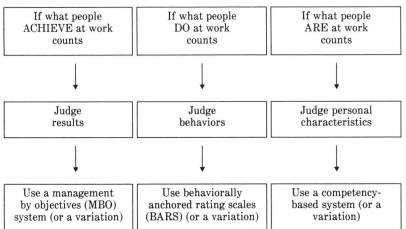

methods for determining performance standards, the method used must be relevant in the context in which it will be used. That is, performance standards must be helpful in setting and communicating performance expectations, directing effort toward successful performance, providing performance-related feedback, solving performance problems, and linking performance to rewards. Skill and practice are needed, but setting standards gets easier when manager and subordinate begin to describe achievements, behaviors, and characteristics required.

Performance appraisal standards and judgments (ratings) must pass certain legal tests. Specific job-related descriptions of performance are appropriate. Rating personnel characteristics—what people are—is neither illegal nor invalid, despite the problems typically associated with trait-based rating systems. The laws do not say personal characteristics such as initiative, dependability, interpersonal skill, or tact do not help determine success—managers know they do and use them—but rather that these characteristics require unambiguous, consistently applied, well-communicated, job-relevant illustrations and definitions. Developing a set of competencies is often a useful approach, as well as a valid one.[1]

Policy problems

Even in organizations where careful attention has been given to identifying measures, setting performance standards, and reducing subjectivity and bias in human judgment, the performance appraisal system may be ineffective if its results are not used or are applied inconsistently (see Figure 1). Solutions involve policies that mandate the use of performance appraisal results as a rationale for

Figure 4.   Performance appraisal (PA) systems fail to recognize the realities of managerial work.

The reality of managerial work is:		Performance appraisal (PA) systems require:
• Numerous activities of short duration • *Ad hoc* informal interactions • A penchant for the nonroutine and for variety • Interest in taking decisive action • Effectiveness due to legitimate authority and supervisory role • Low priority and little importance attached to administrative or personnel tasks and systems	**?**	• Advance planning • Formal sessions, meetings, interviews • Prescribed systems, schedules, forms • Impact of PA results questionable, indirect • Take role of coach or counselor and of equal participation in discussions • Sponsored and designed by administrative/personnel/ human resource development staffs

Source: Adapted from M.W. McCall and D.L. DeVries, *Appraisal in Context: Clashing with Organizational Realities* (Center for Creative Leadership, 1977). See also L.S. Baird, R.W. Beatty, and C.E. Schneier, *The Performance Appraisal Sourcebook* (Human Resource Development Press, 1982).

reward administration, promotion, job assignment, and training. Those workers given the highest evaluations must receive certain performance-contingent rewards. Just as important, those managers who assess and develop their subordinates effectively, using the performance appraisal system as a tool, should be considered successful managers and rewarded appropriately. If human resource decisions are not tied to the results of the appraisal through a set of well-articulated and enforced policies, the performance appraisal system becomes a relic, not a management tool.

Reality problems

The measurement and judgment problems discussed above can be alleviated through various techniques relating to design of performance appraisal formats and training of raters, respectively. However, the policy issues associated with the transition from performance appraisal to performance management require forceful, committed management, trust in the accuracy of performance appraisal results, and a clear sense of purpose for the performance appraisal system.

What remains as a considerable deterrent to performance appraisal system effectiveness, however, does not relate to psychomet-

Figure 5.   Performance appraisal (PA) systems fail to recognize the realities of organization culture.

The reality of organization culture is:	Performance appraisal (PA) systems require:
• Ever-smaller variance in performance levels for upper-level positions • Little time and resources available for administrative tasks • Seniority and loyalty rewarded • Success (and failure) often a function of numerous, complex interdependent relationships • Definitions of success (and failure) difficult to develop and subject to disagreement • Performance expectations, levels, and priorities change rapidly in a dynamic job environment	• Variance in performance levels necessary for reward allocation • Considerable time and resources • Performance rewarded • A single individual's evaluation is sought • Accuracy, consistency, equity, and relative objectivity necessary • Current information in order to retain credibility

? (between the columns)

Source: Adapted from M.W. McCall and D.L. DeVries, *Appraisal in Context: Clashing with Organizational Realities* (Center for Creative Leadership, 1977). See also L.S. Baird, R.W. Beatty, and C.E. Schneier, *The Performance Appraisal Sourcebook* (Human Resource Development Press, 1982).

ric properties of scales, information-processing characteristics of raters, or clarity of policies governing the system, but rather to failure to recognize the realities of managerial work and organizational culture or environment. Performance appraisal systems often clash with the way managers perform their tasks on a day-to-day basis, what degree of control they have, and other realities related to organizational life (Figure 1).

As Figure 4 indicates, performance appraisal systems typically require managers to plan extensively (e.g., setting objectives), interact formally with others (e.g., in formal performance review sessions), adhere to prescribed systems (e.g., completing forms at a certain time each year), and take specific actions (e.g., promotion, pay increase). Performance appraisal also requires managers to relinquish the "superior" role to some extent in order to accept the "coach" role or to allow for participation in goal-setting or performance feedback discussions. Managers may not view their role as including such administrative or personnel functions as performance appraisal; there are HRD staff specialists for these activities. In conflict with these performance appraisal requirements, studies of managerial work indicate that most managers prefer the nonroutine, possess less than complete control over such decisions as promotion, and engage in activities of short duration.[2] It is no wonder they seldom embrace a performance appraisal system—it clashes with the realities of their work and what they enjoy about their jobs.

Figure 5 shows that the effective operation of an appraisal system often conflicts with the typical organization's culture. Variance in performance levels decreases as we move up the hierarchy. A "natural selection" process, while certainly not foolproof, allows the best performers to reach the top. Yet performance appraisal systems may not be very useful if everyone receives high ratings. How can people be rewarded differentially? A seniority system rewards long tenure and loyalty, while a performance appraisal rewards performance. Much success or failure in organizations cannot be traced to a single individual. Yet performance appraisal typically evaluates a single person. Further, objective measures of desired performance and/or those easily agreed upon often do not exist. Yet performance appraisal requires agreement on the definition of successful performance and its indicators. In short, performance appraisal often clashes with the way organizations actually work; no wonder performance appraisals often don't work.

Toward performance management

An examination of performance appraisal system problems, symptoms, and potential cures provides many answers as to why performance appraisal seldom works. What those designing, implementing, evaluating, and using performance appraisal systems in organizations must realize is that such systems cannot be successful unless they are consistent with the realities of managerial work and organizational environments. They must be "user-friendly" and "customer-driven." They must be integrated into the day-to-day activities of managers to help them solve real problems.

An increasing number of organizations have found that appraisal systems are effective if they enhance the superior-subordinate relationship by allowing for frequent communication, specification of expectations, accurate evaluations, and problem solving. It is a *management* cycle, not an appraisal cycle, that facilitates high performance.

1. Schneier, C.E. & Beatty, R.W. (1984). Designing a legally defensible performance appraisal system. In M. Cohen and R. Golembiewski (eds.). *Public Personnel Update.* Marcel Deliker.

2. Mintzberg, H. (1973). *The nature of managerial work.* Harper and Row.

Appraisal without Form-Filling

Gordon Anderson, Ed Young, and David Hulme

More and more organisations are adopting formal systems of performance appraisal, especially for employees at supervisory and management levels. Although the objectives of performance appraisal are accepted as being praiseworthy and utilitarian, it is well documented that the great majority of schemes have not lived up to expectations.

In this article we examine two issues that can determine whether or not a scheme operates effectively. The first is the potential conflict between the objective of developing employees' knowledge, skills and attitudes. Although many organisations have attempted to resolve this possible conflict in the design of their appraisal systems, research evidence suggests that schemes which are strongly future-oriented and which place primary emphasis on development goals are more effective and enduring.

Often little more than lip service is given to establishing what the priorities are: although the importance of development is frequently recognised, that is not necessarily reflected fully in the scheme's design and implementation. A simple system—such as that we examine in this article—which focuses directly on future development objectives can prove more acceptable to all parties and therefore be more likely to contribute to organisational effectiveness.

The second, more radical issue is whether performance appraisal requires the regular production of *written* evaluations of employees. In all the definitions of formal appraisal, committing it to writing is stated either explicitly or implicitly, but our contention

Reprinted with permission from the February 1987 issue of *Personnel Management*, published by Personnel Publications Limited, London.

is that "paperless performance appraisal," focused on a limited number of specific objectives, overcomes many of the traditional difficulties and opens up new alternatives for the use of appraisal.

These issues are examined by means of a case study of an experiment in performance appraisal carried out recently by a major British public sector organisation, the Strathclyde Passenger Transport Executive (SPTE), which is responsible for running the municipal bus service in the Glasgow area. At the time of writing it operates a fleet of 900 buses and has around 3,500 employees, 225 of whom are clerical and managerial.

There was no machinery for the appraisal of employee performance in the SPTE until 1984, when the SPTE's training officer made proposals—which were adopted—to implement an employee appraisal system on a pilot basis. Initially the system was aimed at administrative, professional and managerial employees, though its design was such that if it was successful it could be extended to accommodate craft and manual employees. The scheme's objectives were future-oriented, namely:

1. To improve organisational effectiveness by encouraging the setting of job targets jointly by employees and their managers, against which future performance can be assessed; by encouraging managers to consider and determine with their employees what additional skill requirements are necessary to meet present job demands, and future job demands arising from, for example, changes in technology and legislation; and by encouraging managers to consider employee succession

2. To give employees a better appreciation of their managers' expectations of their performance and, at the same time, acquaint managers with subordinates' expectations of them

3. To alert managers to constraints which may be inhibiting employee performance

4. To improve employee job satisfaction through the activation of the first three objectives.

The primary objective was to improve performance in the present job. There has been no intention to link the performance appraisal scheme to pay or to other tangible rewards or penalties. The purposes of the scheme were set out in a list prepared for the briefing of managers (Figure 1).

An almost "paperless" approach was envisaged from the beginning. There has been no intention, nor is there now, to introduce formal appraisal documentation. The scheme is quite different from totally informal performance appraisal, in that it does require managers to hold appraisal interviews with each of their employees on a regular basis. The pilot scheme operates bi-annually and thereafter

Figure 1. Purposes of the SPTE appraisal scheme.

1. To review what a job holder has achieved over a given period and to examine the causes of success, but primarily of failure, in order to identify 'training needs.'
2. To stimulate and discuss ideas about what could be done to improve the results achieved.
3. To help the job holder analyse strengths and weaknesses and to relate them to performance.
4. To strengthen the job holder's personal commitment to the job.
5. To make the job holder aware of the link between present job performance and career development.
6. To strengthen the understanding between the job holder and the 'manager.'
7. To discuss and resolve any anxiety, uncertainty or misapprehension the job holder may have.
8. To obtain feed-back on how effectively the job holder has been managed.
9. To ensure that the job holder has a clear idea of how 'management' views performance and contribution to the work of the department.
10. To ensure that where the results of the appraisal indicated that a person should be relocated, action is taken to ensure that the person may make the fullest contribution to the organisation.
11. To enable 'management' and the job holder to agree on a number of objectives to be achieved in the coming period against which performance may be measured during the next appraisal.
12. To create the base from which a successful management development program may spring.

annually, except for employees with up to two years' service, for whom appraisal is bi-annual.

Appraisers and appraisees are encouraged to note targets agreed and other action points emerging from the appraisal discussions, but these are confidential to the parties concerned, with no formal recording or reporting to central personnel required. The only formal requirements are that the managers involved should indicate to the training officer that interviews have taken place by the dates agreed and provide the training officer with a note of the training and development requirements for individual employees if any arise and are agreed by the parties.

The aim is to make the system as simple and effective as possible. It is felt that employees will be more positive when it is made clear that there will be no enduring documentation recording 'ratings' and 'evaluative comment.' Equally managers would respond more positively, since the scheme frees them from the reporting requirements that characterise most appraisal schemes and emphasises only the need for noting items of importance—targets, action points, and training needs. It was also anticipated that the simple nature of the scheme would minimise the administrative and co-ordinating demands on the personnel and training departments—a feature of performance appraisal overlooked in many organisations.

It was decided to introduce the pilot scheme in two organisational divisions within the SPTE, namely industrial relations and finance. After one round of appraisal interviews in the two selected areas, it was considered likely that sufficient data and experience would be acquired to enable the SPTE to assess whether to abandon the scheme, modify it or extend it to other areas of the organisation. The plan was that, if the initial pilot study validated the system, the appraisal scheme would be extended to cover white-collar and managerial staff in two other organisational divisions, operations and engineering. The third and final phase would be the extension of the scheme to similar categories of staff in units, i.e., in the various depots and garages.

The SPTE's training officer conducted briefing sessions for those employees who would be appraisees only. These sessions covered the philosophy of performance appraisal, the SPTE's approach to performance appraisal, how an appraisee should prepare for an appraisal interview, the responsibilities of employees and their managers, and the likely benefits for the employee.

Two of the authors, both at the time members of staff at Strathclyde Business School, together with the training officer ran a two-day training course in September 1984 for the senior managers in the pilot areas who would be appraisers only.

Many employees would be both appraisee and appraiser, since a person was always to be appraised by his or her *immediate* supervisor, and further two-day courses were conducted for these middle managers by the training officer.

These courses focused on, first, the philosophy of performance appraisal, and the objectives and methods of the SPTE's approach and, secondly, preparing for appraisal interviews and conducting appraisal interviews, including practice role-playing sessions.

All appraisers were issued with guidelines (Figure 2) to ensure an orderly and systematic approach to the preparation and information-gathering phase, to target-setting, to interview techniques, and to considering employee potential and future manpower issues. Appraisers were encouraged to undertake self-appraisal before their interviews, and a check-list of 'thought-starters' to encourage self-appraisal was issued to appraisers and appraisees alike (Figure 3). The 'paperless' approach is applied to this part of the process too, with no formal self-appraisal document being used.

In the first three months of 1985, all 110 employees in the finance and industrial relations departments were subject to perfor-

Figure 2. Check-list for appraisers.

Job content
Are you entirely sure that you have a thorough knowledge of the content of the appraisee's job description?

Check it anyway!

Discuss the range of duties of the appraisee and agree that your view of the content of the job is the same as the appraisee's. If necessary, negotiate out variances.

Targets—past (as applicable)
Examine the job targets which were set during the last appraisal interview.

Have the targets been achieved in whole or in part?

If they've been achieved in part, what was the reason for the degree of failure?

Was the cause of failure the fault of the appraisee?

Can the cause of the failure be eliminated?

Individual work behaviour
Consider individual facets of the appraisee's capability. Highlight and discuss only those both above and below the norm: numerical ability; linguistic ability; reliability in work; judgment; ambition; conduct; discipline; adaptability; determination; acceptance of responsibility.

What advice would you give to rectify those below the norm?

What advice would you give so that the appraisee may better exploit those above the norm?

What action can you take personally to aid the above two points?

---

mance appraisal. After that an evaluation of the newly introduced performance appraisal pilot scheme was undertaken by interviewing a randomly selected 20 percent sample of all appraisees. All interviewees were also invited to complete a questionnaire.

The 22 interviews were conducted by the training officer, and 20 of those interviewed also completed and anonymously returned the questionnaires. Findings from the perceptions of the appraisees included:

Period of notice and preparation   In the main positive responses were recorded: 80 percent had received two or more days' notice of the appraisal interview (five days' minimum had been recommended); 80 percent of appraisees indicated that they had prepared for their appraisal interviews; and 90 percent felt the period of notice given had been adequate for their preparations.

Figure 2. Continued.

Management skills (as applicable)
Consider the appraisee's ability with the basic management skills: 'planning'; 'organising'; 'delegation'; 'communications'; 'insight/motivation.' Highlight and discuss those below the norm.

What advice would you give to rectify those below the norm?

What action can you take personally to aid this?

Technical skills (as applicable)
Discuss the appraisee's application of technical/professional skills. Is he 'extremely competent?' Is he 'inept?'

If he is 'inept,' why, and what could be done to rectify?

Management potential
Discuss principal strengths and weaknesses of the appraisee.

Has the appraisee's value to the PTE increased or decreased since the last appraisal?

Is the appraisee a round peg in a square hole? Is there a round hole elsewhere?

Does the appraisee have a talent of particular note which would be of value to the PTE if exploited?

Discuss what preparation the appraisee needs to fit him for promotion.

What can you (the appraiser) do on a practical level to assist the appraisee realise his potential?

General discussion
Throw the conversation open to general discussion. Clear the air as necessary.

Promote a successful working relationship.

Location and interview conditions   All appraisees in the sample expressed satisfaction with the interview conditions and locations. There were no problems regarding privacy and interruptions.

The interview process   Most of the measures of the interview process yielded highly positive responses. Only 5 percent said they had been told anything about their job performance that had come as a surprise to them. Ninety percent described the general tone of their appraisal interviews as 'helpful,' 'relaxed' or 'friendly,' indicating a generally supportive approach on the part of appraisers.

Although 95 percent of appraisees felt the length of their interview had been 'about right,' wide variations in interview length appear to have occurred. Forty percent said that their interview had lasted half an hour or less; 35 percent said it had lasted between half an hour and an hour; 15 percent said it had lasted between one and

Figure 3. "Thought starters" for self-appraisal.

The following is a list of questions which members of staff might care to ask themselves in preparation for their appraisal interview with their supervisor. The questions cover the range of topics which will be discussed at the interview, and if some thought is given to the answers, the discussions will be so much easier.

1. What are the main tasks, in order of importance, which you are required to perform?
2. What aspects of your job do you do best?
3. What aspects of your job do you do least well?
4. What have you accomplished during the last 6–12 months?
5. With regard to your present job, what do you hope to accomplish over the next 6–12 months?
6. Do you think that you have a complete understanding of the requirements of your job? If not, of what are you unsure?
7. Are there any problems outside your control which have reduced your ability to perform your job?
8. What training do you think would help you to perform your job more effectively?
9. Do you have any skills or talents which are not being used to the full in your present job?
10. Are there any parts of your job which you think should be altered in any way for any reason?
11. Is there any particular career within the organisation which you would like to follow if you were given the chance?

---

two hours, and 10 percent said their interview had been between two and four hours long.

These, of course, are the recollections of the appraisee and may not be the actual times, but clearly these results warrant further investigation. Despite the satisfaction expressed by appraisees, the danger of superficiality in the level of appraisal discussions seems to be apparent in terms of the large number of interviews which lasted less than 30 minutes. The results can be compared with the findings of a recent IPM survey which shows 30–60 minutes as the most common length of appraisal interview among nonmanagerial employees and one to two hours among managerial employees.[1]

All appraisees in the sample felt they had been given adequate freedom to put forward their views in the interview. Conflict was indicated as having occurred in 25 percent of the interviews. Again this is an issue which calls for further investigation about the nature of the conflict and whether it had in fact been resolved. Only two respondents claimed to have experienced conflict which had been unresolved at the end of the interview.

Target-setting   The sample of appraisees was divided on whether job targets for the appraisee had been agreed on a joint basis at the interview; 50 percent said 'yes' and 50 percent said 'no.'

Identification of training needs   Again there was an even split, with 50 percent indicating that training needs had been identified and agreed at the interview and the other 50 percent saying not. There is no evidence that the two 50 percents were the same for this and for target-setting.

Retention of the scheme   The great majority of appraisees in the sample felt the system should be retained. Some of the individual comments from the interviews reinforced this view, but also point out some dangers:

"I was not happy about it before, but having been subject to the system I have changed my mind."
"The confidentiality is good; you get down to the real issues because of it."
"We are better with the system than without it."

Some of the reservations were expressed as follows:

" 'Appraisal' was really just a chat."
"The boss was only going through the motions."
"Keep the system but put things that are agreed on record so that they cannot be twisted at a later date."

Arguably these comments (positive and negative) could be as much an indication of the appraisers' managerial styles as a qualitative statement about the appraisal system.

To complete the initial evaluation process, the training officer conducted a meeting with the 20 appraisers to elicit their views and to give them an opportunity to comment on the views expressed by appraisees. Without exception the managers involved expressed positive views about the pilot scheme, and recommended its retention and extention within the SPTE. Some managers admitted that they had not always identified training needs or, if they had, may not have communicated these as they should have to the training officer. This was an issue which they felt could readily be rectified in the next round of appraisals. Some managers indicated that, in identifying employeee training needs, they had been able to deal with these through coaching and on-the-job training, without needing help from the training department.

Clearly some of the ambiguities and unanswered questions from the initial evaluation merit further investigation, but, in the light of the many problems encountered by a wide range of organisations in implementing performance appraisal, the success of this pilot exercise is high. The positive nature of the results are all the more surprising, given the uncertainty of the environment within which passenger transport executives, including SPTE, are currently operating. Because of legislation aimed at increasing competition among bus services, many SPTE employees are anxious about the prospects for continued employment, so that more negative and defensive views might have been expected.

Although managers and employees expressed general satisfaction with interview processes (relaxed atmosphere, freedom to express views, supportive relationships) there is clearly scope for improving the outcomes of the appraisal interviews, with no job targets for employees being set and no training and development needs identified in 50 percent of cases. There was also a general failure on the part of managers to inform the training officer fully of the training needs of their subordinates, though, as noted above, this can be easily corrected. This issue of positive interview processes associated with less positive outcomes has been detected in other recent studies.[2]

While the paperless approach to performance appraisal has many virtues, there is the danger that, without the discipline of documentation to think through and complete, some interviews may border on the superficial. Further investigation of this crucially important issue is needed. Regular monitoring of both appraiser and appraisee attitudes towards appraisal and the effectiveness of its implementation is seen as a necessary condition for the operation of this type of appraisal scheme.

The scheme has now been widened to include other white-collar and managerial staff. It has yet to be introduced for craft and manual workers, although this remains a long-term objective.

A major issue will be how to sustain momentum. Further investigation is clearly required to answer the crucial question of how far the initial positive response was due to the fact that, generally, a sound approach methodologically was adopted in introducing the scheme and how far it was due to its special 'paperless' features.

Sufficient evidence has been gathered to suggest it represents an approach which other organisations could usefully consider. Although applied in this situation to white-collar and managerial staff, our view is that it is an approach which, because of its simple and straightforward nature, is worthy of careful consideration in organisations that are contemplating a revision of their appraisal practices. In particular, the simplicity and lack of paperwork may well commend itself in situations where appraisal is being extended to employees at lower levels in the hierarchy, including blue-collar workers.

1. Long, P. *Performance appraisal revisited*, IPM, 1986.
2. Anderson, G.C. and Barnett, J.C.

'Nurse appraisal in practice,' *Health Service Journal*, 30 October 1986.

Performance Appraisal: A Case in Points

Ted Cocheu

"Hey Harry, have a seat! Thanks for coming by on such short notice. I got this reminder from personnel the other day and I thought, since I had a few free minutes in my schedule this afternoon, we could go ahead and polish off your annual performance appraisal.

"The bottom line, Harry, is that I think you're doing a pretty good job. You usually get things in on time and the quality of your work is really not too bad.

"There are also a few minor problems I need to bring to your attention. First is your attitude. You don't seem like the old Harry I once knew—always anxious to go the extra mile if necessary.

"You look like you just can't wait to hit the door at five o'clock these days. That doesn't look good to the guys in the front office, so keep it in mind in terms of your career here.

"Next, remember that report you sent to the Board of Directors last quarter? Well, it had several pages miscollated and that really embarrassed the old man. I never said anything, because I didn't want to get on your back, but you really need to be more careful on these things.

"There are a few other things I could bring up but, like I said, you're doing a pretty good job and I just want to see you put in a little more effort in the future. That's about it Harry. Any questions before you sign the form here on the bottom?"

Sound familiar? Performance appraisal—it's something every manager must do and few do well. No matter how often you emphasize the importance of proper appraisals, most supervisors continue to treat the process as a major imposition rather than as a vital part of their jobs.

You may have resorted to exhortations from executives, changing the appraisal forms and conducting mandatory training on the subject.

You may even have experimented with the latest and greatest appraisal techniques as they have drifted in and out of vogue, such as management by objectives (MBO), behaviorally anchored rating scales (BARS), and others.

What's next? What can be done to improve this unfortunate situation?

One corporation's response was to completely overhaul its appraisal system, a change that began by recognizing that the existing system was inadequate. Implementing the new system involved careful study of the alternatives, establishment of priorities, development of a new system, and, finally, implementation.

Each of the steps offers valuable insights into the appraisal process, and the experiences of the system's development can be used by any company to improve its appraisal process.

A task force was developed to identify the problems

The process began when both management and employees at a multinational electronics company had become extremely frustrated with the company's performance appraisal system (or lack of one) and developed a task force to recommend and develop a better approach.

Top management had evaluated the company's existing practices and defined the following problems:

1. Each division was using different approaches, forms and rating scales. These inconsistencies resulted in numerous inequities and made it difficult to evaluate people for promotions across organizational lines.

2. Although the different rating scales made comparisons difficult, it was also clear from looking at the records that the ratings were seriously skewed toward the high end. This skew made it difficult to differentiate between levels of performance, and it was unclear who the exceptional performers were.

3. Most of the techniques used were based on traits or relied on retrospective statements of what had been accomplished during the evaluation period. Those tendencies made it impossible for anyone other than the immediate manager to look at the appraisals and assess an individual's performance. It was also difficult to tie individual performance to organizational goals.

4. Appraisals were normally completed at the end of the period, becoming a necessary evil in the process of justifying salary increases and promotions, and were not used to manage performance on an ongoing basis.
5. Performance appraisals in general were one-way communications from managers to employees, rather than a conversation in which employees play a responsible role.

The task force, composed of senior HRD and line managers, was commissioned to study these problems, survey the literature and practices in competitive companies, and make recommendations. The members were given three months in which to research, present their findings, and recommend a course of action.

The task force divided the initial workload into five areas, with the following findings:

A study of current practices and methodologies throughout the company   As anticipated, the study of existing methodology revealed a diversity of appraisal approaches were being used, ranging from simple adjective checklists to fairly elaborate MBO systems. No particular approach seemed to predominate. In addition, the task force determined that job descriptions were badly out of date or absent and people did not have a clear understanding of their responsibilities.

A survey of what key executives, managers and individuals wanted to see and not see in a new or revised system   A survey was administered to determine what members of various groups wanted to see in a new system.

To summarize, executives wanted to see a standardized approach they could use to compare people across organizational lines. They also wanted to be able to clearly distinguish between three categories of performance: outstanding, meeting expectations and below expectations.

Managers and supervisors, on the other hand, emphasized their need for a relatively easy and efficient procedure. They repeatedly emphasized upper management's unrealistic demands.

Predictably, employees wanted to have their performance judged fairly by their bosses. This meant they wanted to know what was expected of them in advance and what criteria would be used to evaluate them.

A survey of the practices at competitive firms and other companies of similar size and diversity   A review of the forms and supporting documents used by a representative number of companies in the industry showed diversity in the approaches being taken.

The task force found innumerable methods being used, but objective-based systems, in various forms, were by far the most common. Representatives from companies were interviewed, and several had recently implemented or upgraded their MBO systems.

Consultation with the legal staff to determine the current status and trends of EEO-related and other legal issues Clearly, the most critical legal issues regarding performance appraisal systems, as with any employment policies or procedures, are job-relatedness and consistency of application. The criteria against which an employee's performance is evaluated must be directly related to the requirements of the job.

Ideally, companies should have accurate, written job requirements, responsibilities and/or behaviors for each position, along with explicit criteria that describe different levels of performance. In addition, the evaluation procedure must be consistently applied to all employees so that no bias or preferential treatment can be demonstrated.

The new system had six objectives

The task force's findings were summarized and presented to the management steering group in a meeting designed to develop a common understanding of the underlying issues and formulate specific objectives for the new system.

After heated discussions, six core objectives were agreed upon, along with the rationale for each:

1. A single company-wide system Although several well-developed approaches were already in place in the divisions, the steering group felt that the company had to have a uniform approach across organizational lines.

The advantages were recognized as:

- The overall company identity could be restated and reinforced.
- Interorganizational comparisons of individual performers would be facilitated.
- Employee records would be consistent when people transferred between divisions.
- Implementation and training would be simplified.

2. An objective-based system A modified MBO approach was selected for the following reasons:

- The group felt strongly that managers needed a means to help plan and communicate employee performance requirements formally.

- Top management wanted a vehicle to tie individual performance at every level of the organization to company-wide objectives.
- The system had to work and be job-related in the absence of up-to-date job descriptions, and setting specific objectives for each person would allow for this.
- Management wanted to focus on outcomes rather than behaviors and, therefore, felt that a BARS approach was not appropriate (in addition to it being cumbersome and expensive to implement).

3. Active employee participation   The group wanted to change the nature of the process from a one-way communication from the supervisor to the subordinate to one in which employees were actively involved. Some of the specific considerations included:

- Employees would take personal accountability for achieving objectives they helped set.
- The quality and frequency of job-related communications between managers and subordinates would improve if they had to agree on the objectives.
- The person performing the work usually has the best knowledge of the opportunities and the constraints surrounding his or her job.
- The negotiation process should bring about performance objectives that would be demanding yet realistic.
- The process would result in personal growth and a greater degree of employee self-management.

4. Periodic review and update   A major problem the company had was that performance was typically reviewed on an annual basis without formal discussions throughout the period to monitor progress and spot problems.

In addition, the electronics industry is dynamic and the need for re-direction is continual. The group felt the new system would have to explicitly deal with these problems and encourage periodic performance updates.

5. Differentiated performance levels   Top management wanted to allocate rewards based on performance and needed to be able to clearly differentiate between superior, average and below average employees. The new system had to provide meaningful distinctions and avoid the tendency to skew ratings toward the high end.

6. Employee development   In addition to being an appraisal device, the committee felt the new system should also provide for and

---

**Performance Planning
and Evaluation**

Employee Information	Employee Name
	Review Period: From _____ To _____
	Current Position Title
	Date Assigned to Current Position _____ Reports to _____
	Group/Organization
	Location _____ Region/District (Names) _____

Overview	The Performance Planning and Evaluation Process has three pieces. This form will be used to document each step of the process.
	• **Performance Planning**— Step 1 of this form will be used to state the key results, objectives, and priorities the manager and employee mutually agree upon.
	• **Performance Management**— This involves the day-to-day coaching for improved performance as well as informal and formal progress reviews. The formal progress review will be documented in Step 2.
	• **Performance Evaluation**—Steps 3-5 will be used for the Annual Performance Evaluation which includes the objectives review, performance review, and the overall evaluation.

Descriptions of Ratings Used in Evaluating Performance	Exceeded Job Requirements	7	Performance exceeded the requirements of the job in all major areas and significant work above and beyond the responsibilities of the job was achieved.
		6	Performance exceeded the requirements of the job in several important areas.
	Achieved Job Requirements	5	Performance met job requirements in all important areas with extra effort evident in quality, quantity, timeliness or some other important dimensions of performance.
		4	Performance met job requirements in all important areas.
		3	Performance met job requirements but improvement would be desirable in one or more areas.
	Below Job Requirements	2	Performance was below job requirements in one or more important areas and immediate improvement will be required.
		1	Performance is significantly below requirements of the job in several important areas. Reassignment or termination should be considered.

---

encourage employee development. Although management wanted to separate career planning from the appraisal process, they did want managers to take greater responsibility for coaching and counseling employees on their current assignments.

The new system integrated planning with evaluation

With these objectives as the foundation, the task force began developing an approach that would satisfy all of the requirements. The literature and the documentation from other companies were re-

Step 1
Performance Plan

The Performance Plan is to be completed at the beginning of the review period and should reflect the mutually understood key results areas and agreed-upon performance objectives for the period. In determining "Relative Importance," compare the objectives and assign a rank to each according to its priority, emphasis in terms of time and effort, and significance of results expected. The total for this column is equal to approximately 60% of the Overall Evaluation (Step 5).

Key Result Areas: List the major results or outcomes for your position. For examples of key result areas see the booklet, "Performance Planning and Evaluation."	Objectives: List the specific objectives expected to be accomplished in the coming review period for each key result area. State objectives in measureable terms and include what is to be accomplished, by what date, at what cost, quality, or other relevant factors.	Relative Importance

Manager's Signature   Employee's Signature

viewed again and the best insights and elements were integrated into the new system.

After a series of meetings and numerous revisions, the task force agreed the new system would be called "Performance Planning and Evaluation" (PP&E), a seven-point rating scale would be used, and the system would have five major steps.

Rating scale   The key to the entire system is the rating scale, developed around several key issues:

Step 2 Progress Review	Step 3 Performance Evaluation	
	This is the year end formal performance evaluation. When rating the results achieved for each objective, take into consideration the difficulty, complexity, and other factors which	influenced the results obtained. Use the numerical rating scale on the front page to evaluate the employee's performance on each objective. See instructions below. Then determine the overall objectives rating by considering the ratings and relative importance of each objective.
Interim Progress Review: The employee and supervisor should meet as often as needed to discuss objectives, however one formal review should be held, at least on a semi-annual basis, to review progress toward objectives. The objectives and their priorities should be modified and updated as necessary. Date of Interim Review_____	**Results and Achievements:** Describe in a brief and factual manner the specific results achieved for each objective in Step 1. Comment briefly on what most influenced your evaluation of each. Include any appropriate suggestions for improvement.	**Performance Rating**
Manager's Signature		
Employee's Signature	Overall Objectives Rating _____	

Terminology   The term "job requirements" was chosen as opposed to "objectives" because an aggressive objective could well surpass the normal requirements of the position.

This encourages people to set challenging objectives and not understate them. The terms, "exceeded," "achieved" and "below" are applied to the extent to which employees meet specific expectations, rather than the previously used, and vague, terms "superior," "average," and "below average."

Step 4
Performance Factors

The Performance Factors describe how the employee goes about achieving objectives. Give specific examples of observed behavior. Rate the Human Resources Development section if the employee supervises others. The Human Resource rating will generally account for one half of the total overall rating in this section. However, for individuals with only one or two employees, the evaluator may choose to factor this at a slightly lesser percent. Use the rating scale on the front page to determine which rating best describes the performance for each factor.

Factors	Strengths — Specific Examples	Area for Development — Specific Examples	Performance Rating
Organizing, Planning, and Decision Making: Anticipates and systematically analyzes problems and opportunities; identifies key tasks and critical sequential steps; establishes priorities, schedules and contingency plans; analyzes reasonable alternatives and takes action in a timely manner; efficiently allocates and manages resources; demonstrates sound judgment.			
Job Commitment: Willingly accepts responsibility and performs expected and unexpected tasks; demonstrates initiative, tenacity in completing tasks and solving problems; willingly exerts extra effort when necessary to get the job done.			
Knowledge of Field: Demonstrates familiarity with, and the application of, current technology, techniques, and trends (both inside and outside Burroughs) that pertain to assigned work responsibilities.			
Communications: Expresses ideas and concerns clearly and persuasively, both orally and in writing; is proficient and confident making formal presentations; listens effectively.			
Teamwork: Works and interacts with others to accomplish overall group goals; willingly works with group decisions; considers suggestions from others; is sensitive to the needs of people; solicits feedback.			
Factor Rating 1-5			
Human Resource Development: Coaches and counsels employees to sustain and improve job performance. Works with employees to develop their potential and increase their value to the Company. Motivates employees through fair and equitable management practices, including selection, promotion, salary administration and performance evaluation. Takes visible and meaningful action to recruit and develop females and minorities*			

*U.S. employees only

Human Resource Rating (employees without management and professional direct reports should not be rated on this factor.)

Overall Factors Rating _____

Categories The scale was first divided into three major categories as noted above. Task force studies showed that people can easily distinguish between performance that exceeds, achieves or is below job requirements. Once those broad distinctions have been made, it is then possible for raters to make subtle distinctions within those categories.

Definitions Each level of performance, from one to seven, is given

---

Step 5
Overall Evaluation

The rating of performance in relation to Objectives (Step 3) is worth approximately 60% and the rating on relevant performance factors is worth approximately 40% of the Overall Evaluation. Using these guidelines the manager determines an overall rating. The Overall Evaluation should be interpreted using the Descriptions of Ratings on the front page.

Guideline — The overall evaluation should be determined by looking at the three pieces of the evaluation with these approximate percents.

Overall Objective Evaluation	60%	
Performance Factors 1-5	20%	
Human Resource Development Factor	20%	

Overall Evaluation

Supervisor's Comments: Provide a brief summary statement which characterizes the employee's overall performance and supports your rating.

Employee's Comments: Do you understand how your performance was evaluated? Provide other comments as desired.

(Your signature does not necessarily signify your agreement with the appraisal. it simply means the appraisal has been discussed with you.)

	Employee's Signature	Date
Immediate Manager (Reviewer) (Print)	Signature	Date
Second Level Manager (Print)	Signature	Date

---

a specific definition (rather than a label, such as superior) to give the appraiser a solid basis for assigning ratings.

Performance planning   The performance planning step is divided into three parts:

Key result areas (KRAs)   In lieu of accurate job descriptions, KRAs were developed to define the major elements of each job type.

Within each key result area, specific objectives could be defined for the upcoming review period.

KRAs remain relatively stable over time, even though objectives normally change according to the business requirements. An example of a set of KRAs for a personnel manager might be: recruitment, compensation, employee relations, training, and personal development.

Objectives The planning step includes standard objective setting, which is familiar in all MBO systems. Employees are encouraged to draft objectives for themselves, based on organizational goals provided by their managers. Managers do the same and then negotiate an agreement both parties feel is challenging but realistic.

Relative importance After setting the objectives for the coming period, managers are then asked to assign priorities to the objectives according to their impact on organizational goals.

Interim progress review The interim review is included for ongoing performance management. Progress toward objectives is noted throughout the period, as are problems. Any changes in the objectives or their priorities are to be formalized whenever they occur.

Performance evaluation The final results are compared to these objectives:

Results and achievements The employee's progress toward the objectives is described as specifically and quantitatively as possible at the end of the review period.

Employees are encouraged to draft their own account of their accomplishments before the review meeting so the manager and employee can share their perceptions in a constructive dialogue.

Performance rating After discussing performance related data, the employee and the manager exchange their numerical evaluations of performance toward each objective.

Managers are encouraged to take a negotiable approach to the meeting and not to finalize any ratings until after the first discussion. Then, considering both the performance ratings on the objectives and the relative importance of each, the manager uses his or her discretion to determine an overall rating for the objectives section. This rating is not intended to be calculated mathematically and is intentionally designed to give the manager latitude.

The rating on objectives is intended to represent 60% of the total rating.

Performance factors   The performance factors section is designed to be more subjective and to be used by managers as a developmental tool.

Factors   The five factors (organizing, planning and decision making; job commitment; knowledge of field; communications; and teamwork) were selected to represent generic skills and abilities applicable to any job. They were also written in such a way as to communicate certain company values, such as teamwork.

This section constitutes 40% of the entire appraisal, and is intended to communicate to employees and managers alike that the way in which work is performed (as opposed to tangible results) is also important.

A sixth factor, human resources development, was included for anyone with direct responsibility for managing people. It is assigned 20% of the total weight of the appraisal (50% of the factors section) and the weighting is intended to emphasize the importance of personnel development to those in management positions.

Strengths and areas for development   The performance factors section includes space for managers to offer balanced feedback to the employee relative to both strengths and weaknesses. Managers are required to provide specific examples of observed behavior.

Performance rating   As with the objectives or planning section, managers are asked to rate each factor and consolidate them into an overall rating for the factors section. Appraisals of managers must account for the combined weighting of the first five factors as a group and the human resources development factor.

Overall evaluation   The results of the first four sections are summarized in the overall evaluation, along with qualitative statements by the manager and employee.

Overall rating   The overall rating for the entire evaluation is determined by taking the ratings from the performance plan and performance factors, multiplying them by 60% and 40% respectively, and adding them together. If the manager and employee reach a basic understanding on the first four sections, then no surprises or disagreements should be expected at the end.

Supervisor's comments   The reviewer is encouraged to provide a narrative or qualitative summary of his or her perceptions of the employee's overall performance and contributions to the organization.

Employee's comments   The employee is encouraged to express in writing how he or she feels about the review, both positively and negatively. The employee can also take this opportunity to make other comments regarding the current assignment.

Success of the system depended on implementation

An implementation plan for the new system was developed as the system was designed. The task force felt no matter now good the system was it would fail if not implemented properly. Therefore, the implementation strategy had three major components:

Phased approach   The system's success depended on a commitment from management at all levels, so the committee chose to test it with managers only for the first year.

The previous forms used to appraise management performance for determining bonuses were replaced with the new system so that managers would become familiar with it.

Only after PP&E had been used to appraise managers for one complete planning and evaluation cycle and the task force felt it had the necessary support was it implemented throughout the organization.

Communication   During the one-year test period, the committee used whatever means it could to publicize the introduction of the new system.

The chairman and president both included references to the system in their verbal and written communication to employees, and they stressed that it is part of an overall program to increase employee involvement in all aspects of their work.

Articles about the system were included in the company newsletter, and it began to become part of the language of the organization even before its full implementation.

Training   A two-day training program was developed to familiarize managers at all levels with the program and help build the necessary skills in setting objectives, using the new rating scale, providing constructive feedback and coaching employees for improved performance.

The program was developed internally, and line managers were used as positive role models in videotaped vignettes. The corporate training department delivered the program to home office executives and trained field human resources managers to deliver the program to managers in their organizations. This train-the-trainer approach had the following advantages:

1. The program was implemented more quickly than would otherwise have been possible.
2. It built the appraisal skills of the human resources managers.

3. It got the human resources community to take local responsibility for the success of the system.

Although not perfect in design or implementation, the PP&E system largely fulfilled the six objectives of the executive committee and made a positive impact on the organization.

Although the ongoing communications process can always be improved, the frequency of formally reviewing and updating objectives during the review period has increased noticeably.

The seven-point scale has helped managers differentiate between levels of performance, and the ratings collectively are closer to being normally distributed than before.

Finally, a careful review of completed PP&E forms indicates that managers are definitely spending more time counseling and developing employees for improved performance.

Difficulties

This success, however, was not without its difficulties and rough spots. Some of the problems encountered, which will probably never be resolved entirely, include:

Management time   The new system is a time-consuming process and requires a lot of work on the part of managers and employees alike. Busy managers who are pulled in too many directions at once continue to find it difficult to spend the time required. This is the result of two problems:

1. Most managers resist delegation and still insist on being involved in the technical aspects of the work—even though it leads to their own ineffectiveness as managers.
2. Being busy simply comes with the territory—managers will always have to juggle several jobs at once and it will never be easy or comfortable.

Employee participation   As noted, managers have a tough time delegating and treating employees as responsible partners in meeting organizational goals. Therefore, many managers continue to unilaterally determine performance objectives rather than negotiate them and, consequently, lose much of the potential commitment they could gain from employees.

Environmental change   Setting objectives in a rapidly changing environment is always somewhat frustrating because objectives tend to become out of date or obsolete quickly.

Managers frequently use this as a justification for not setting or maintaining objectives for their people, but there are some things that can be done to make it easier.

1. Don't see objectives as carved in stone. Write objectives in pencil so they can be updated as necessary.
2. Make employees responsible for bringing it to the attention of management anytime they perceive changes in priorities or direction. Then, all managers have to do is confirm or clarify the current situation.
3. If too many things are changing too rapidly, suggest to managers they shorten the review period from nine to 12 months to six months.

Conclusion

Despite these difficulties, the benefits of the new system to employees and managers were well worth the time and effort required to make the change. Change never comes easily, so it's not surprising the complete success of the PP&E system will have to work its way through the organization over time.

Although the task force felt it was being cautious in estimating that implementation would take two full years, it will certainly take longer. The magnitude and the implications of attempting to make major systems changes should never be underestimated. Although the task is not an easy one, every company can benefit from improving the ways in which the organization plans for and evaluates the performance of its human resources.

Part 3

Managing Employee Performance

Performance Management: Not Just an Annual Appraisal

Kathleen Guinn

"Performance appraisal is not an annual event. For best results, it should be a series of events throughout the year. Effective appraisal is an ongoing activity that should be part of every manager's routine."

How many times have managers been offered that line of pat advice? It's, oh, so familiar . . . and, oh, so confusing—if not downright misleading—to people who are struggling to conduct effective performance appraisals.

Asking managers to make performance appraisal part of their daily routine is asking the impossible. Formidable tasks such as analyzing past performance, assigning ratings, completing appraisal forms and discussing salary increases cannot be done on an "ongoing" basis.

Performance appraisal is not an unimportant or easy management task. But trying to make it a continuous activity only increases confusion and exaggerates its difficulty. Performance appraisal is, and should be, a once-a-year event. It is *performance management,* a different thing altogether, that is and should be a year-round activity.

This is where the alert reader perhaps accuses me of setting up a straw man. People who talk about making performance appraisal an ongoing activity aren't suggesting that evaluation sheets be filled out and ratings assigned and salary discussed every day, you object. And you're right; they aren't suggesting that at all. But by speaking of performance appraisal and performance management as if they're the same process, we cloud an important distinction. And we make two difficult tasks that much more difficult.

The alleged objective of performance appraisal is to produce informed, motivated employees who are committed to improving the effectiveness of their performance—in short, to improving their productivity. Yet there is no proven link between performance appraisal and increased productivity. There is, however, a strong correlation between performance management and increased productivity. Ironically, performance appraisal research clearly establishes that correlation.

Ineffective objectives

The reason we conduct performance appraisals in the first place is that we believe (or claim to believe) that they will accomplish two things:

1. Help employees understand the quality of their current performance and identify what they must do to improve it. Obviously, this objective implies changing employees' behavior.
2. Motivate employees to improve their performance. Again, clearly the implication is behavior change.

Now consider these objectives against what we know about achieving behavioral changes. To be effective in changing behavior, performance feedback must occur as soon as possible after the employee displays the behavior you wish to change. Rapping a puppy on the nose for soiling the rug three months after the event will not make the puppy stop soiling the rug, much less affect its understanding or motivation.

Does this mean that because a formal appraisal occurs months after the actual performance, we have to redefine it to make it something it is not? No. It simply means that a performance-appraisal system is not designed to provide immediate feedback on performance; performance management is.

The difference between the two is analogous to two different but equally important activities in the world of business and finance: financial management and the annual audit. The annual audit benefits managers responsible for the organization's financial performance by providing a "snapshot" of its financial situation that can be studied, analyzed and evaluated. Managers use the event to identify trends in financial performance, build on strengths, develop strategies, solve problems and establish goals. All of these things result in a healthier, stronger organization.

However, the audit itself is not part of the daily process of managing the organization's financial performance. No one would propose that to be effective, the annual audit should be "something that goes on all year . . . a day-in and day-out activity."

Similarly, performance appraisal is only one step in an effective performance-management process. Just like the annual audit, the annual performance appraisal provides a "snapshot" that allows study, analysis and evaluation. Managers use the event to identify trends in performance, build on strengths, develop strategies, solve problems and establish goals. All of these activities are aimed at strengthening employee performance and, consequently, the organization's performance.

Thus, the primary objective of performance appraisal, positioned as a single step in a performance management system, is to provide a data base for planning and targeting changes in future performance. Focusing on this objective also alleviates many of the complaints managers and employees voice about annual performance appraisals (see accompanying sidebar).

The performance management approach

Since performance management occurs on a year-round basis, it can help employees understand the nature and quality of their recent performance, identify what they must do to improve and motivate them to improve. Effective performance management has three basic components: planning, managing and appraising performance.

Performance planning   Performance planning is the process of identifying the desired performance and gaining employees' commitment to perform to those expectations.

Corporate performance is generally described in terms of results: short- and long-term profits, dividends, return on assets and return on investment. Similarly, performance planning focuses on individual results: *what* an individual achieves and, perhaps just as importantly, *how* these results are achieved.

Appraisal forms often recognize the importance of the "how" aspect by addressing areas such as cooperation, initiative and leadership. But managers need to be trained to identify and assess those intangible qualities. Managers also must be able to gain employees' commitment to using desirable behaviors by relating the use of the behaviors to the attainment of specific results: tying the "how" to the "what" during the performance planning phase. Only then can the manager justify subsequent feedback, coaching and appraisal.

Performance planning that clearly identifies the expected results, as well as the behaviors and skills the individual is expected to demonstrate, provides a specific action plan aimed at a clear target. A planning strategy that solicits the active participation of subordinates in the process will help build commitment and minimize conflict in subsequent appraisal discussions.

Performance managing Performance managing is the daily process of working toward the performance expectations established in the planning phase. Together, manager and employee review the employee's performance on a periodic basis. If it's on track or exceeding expectations, the manager provides positive reinforcement to keep performance at a high level (see Figure 1). If performance is lacking, the manager coaches the employee on improving trouble spots. This involves developing strategies *with* the employee to determine appropriate action plans.

Curing the appraisal blues

Performance appraisal systems that are forced into doing double duty as performance management systems are bound to create difficulties for bosses, employees and organizations. By approaching performance appraisal as simply a step in the performance-management approach, however, you can eliminate or at least minimize many of these common problems.

Appraisals are perceived as confrontations. If the objective of performance appraisal is to plan for the next cycle, there is nothing to "confront." Blame for past performance becomes irrelevant. The manager directs the discussion from the perspective of "Here's what was. Now how do we reach our goals for this year?" Focusing on the future helps to minimize defensiveness; it's unnecessary to "defend" what has yet to happen.

Because performance management includes handling poor performance when it occurs, there is no need to reopen lengthy discussions during the appraisal itself. The unacceptable behavior was identified and dealt with; now it is only a part of the data base under consideration. Eliminating the confrontational nature of the performance appraisal creates less anxiety and, thus, more opportunity for collaborating on future actions.

Managers must act as judges of individual worth. While it would be ideal to take ratings out of performance appraisals, that's unlikely to happen as long as they are used to justify salary decisions. Indeed, many progressive companies are tying salary and performance even closer together through pay-for-performance systems. These systems, however, do not *require* "ratings" of performance. They do require clearly established performance goals or objectives, an equally essential part of a performance-management approach.

Nonetheless, when the objective of performance appraisal is to provide a data base for *planning* future performance, ratings are more easily tied to past performance, not the employee's personal worth. In other words, the focus on planning helps the manager aim

---

Coaching on a timely basis eliminates the often unpleasant—and unproductive—"postmortem" aspects of performance appraisal. Problems are handled when action can be taken, also eliminating the "gotcha" element of the appraisal interview. When the manager's role becomes one of coach rather than judge, boss and subordinate can work together to achieve the individual's performance goals, which are, after all. the unit's goals and, ultimately, the organization's goals.

Managers who periodically track and review performance let employees know where they stand; performance-appraisal discussions hold no surprises. Instead, boss and subordinate discuss performance when it actually occurs—the ideal time to affect behavior. The year-end performance review becomes a summary with little or

---

feedback at the behavior and the accomplishments, instead of at the person.

Performance appraisals often are conducted without clear objectives in mind. When managers stop to think why they are doing these appraisals, they come up with vague and confusing reasons—"to create understanding," "to motivate the employee to do better," or even "because I have to." With the performance-management approach, the appraisal is conducted with a single, clearly established objective: to review past performance to provide a data base for planning future performance.

The appraisal focuses on filling out the form. Forms become less important when the objective is to provide a data base for future plans. Since performance management builds a working relationship between the manager and subordinate, the appraisal form becomes simply a convenient job aid for the manager, rather than the structural force for the performance-appraisal discussion.

Performance data is seldom gathered in advance. Performance management helps the boss and subordinate gather data in smaller, more convenient units throughout the year. Sources for tracking results and frequency of review are established when the performance expectations are identified. Review of performance on a monthly or quarterly basis is easier, quicker and usually more accurate because the information is current.

Interim reviews are filed for future reference prior to the yearly performance appraisal. This eliminates the last-minute rush—or more accurately, the desperate attempt—to find data to support general impressions. Because data are readily available, both parties are less likely to drift into subjective general impressions or statements that inevitably provoke emotional reactions.

Clear-cut action plans are not established. When the objective of the appraisal is to plan future performance, it is virtually impossible to walk out of the discussion without an action plan. Clear, specific goals are established for the upcoming performance cycle.

Figure 1. Performance managing.

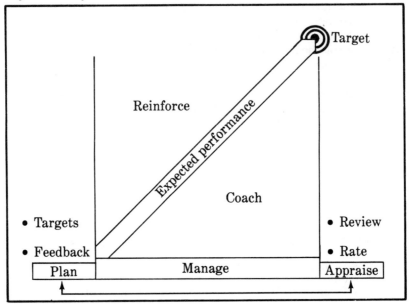

no new information, and discussion focuses on planning for the future performance cycle.

Performance appraisal   Performance appraisal, the final step in the performance-management process, provides the opportunity to step back from day-to-day activities, assess performance trends and plan for the future. Because periodic performance reviews have essentially eliminated any surprises, both boss and employee can anticipate the nature of the discussion and prepare for the meeting accordingly. Career development, a natural outgrowth of this discussion, helps build the employee's commitment and loyalty to the organization, increasing motivation and productivity as well.

The performance appraisal is both the beginning and the end point of performance management. The analysis of past performance provides the basis for planning next year's expectations; at the same time, it "closes the loop" of the current cycle. Employees know what is expected of them and what they need to do to achieve results in the next performance period. The organization knows what results it can expect from employees and what resources are needed to help them achieve those results.

Managing Employee Performance

———————— Dawn Marie Warfle and Linda Hopper

Most managers feel quite comfortable "managing" data, equipment, supplies, and other similar resources. But, when it comes to employee performance, some managers throw up their arms in surrender. One of the great difficulties in managing employee performance is that we cannot proceed without an adequate or appropriate way of *measuring* what we want to manage. This task involves performance planning and establishing appropriate standards of performance, documenting performance, and planning periodic meetings to evaluate progress.

Planning performance management and establishing appropriate standards

Planning for performance management must start with an understanding of what constitutes good performance. Essentially this means that you must understand the functions of each position within your department. Prepare *a list of job tasks* or *activities* for each position. Compare your list with the one prepared by your employee. Discuss and reconcile any differences. Both of you should agree about what the employee actually does on the job.

After compiling a final list of job activities, you and the employee must determine the importance of each activity. Again, it's essential that you both agree on the same order of priorities.

Next, you should discuss performance expectations. This is the time to set specific standards of performance. Everyone needs some means of judging whether a performance is "good," "bad," or "in

Reprinted with permission from *Performance Evaluation: A Manager's Guide to Employee Development*, Training Program (Washington, D.C.: International City Management Association, 1987).

need of improvement." The list of significant job activities indicates what needs to be accomplished, whereas the standards of performance indicate how well the task must be done.

Performance appraisal experts define standards of performance in several ways. This article uses the following definition: "Performance standards describe the level of performance the employee is expected to achieve and/or the objectives the employee is expected to accomplish."[1]

Regardless of which definition you use, once the standards are established by you and your employee, they become the measuring stick for assessing all future performance. Suggestions for writing standards of performance for jobs within local governments will be limited to stating characteristics of standards which have been judged effective:

1. Each job has its own standards.
2. Standards must be realistic. All employees doing the same job should be able to achieve the standards for satisfactory performance.
3. Employees should agree on the standards. After all, it is the employee who is being evaluated on the basis of these standards.
4. Standards should be as objective as possible. Not every standard can be stated in terms of numbers. But if measurement is a realistic option, quantify standards. If not, be as specific as possible.
5. Standards are used to evaluate a person within a particular time frame. Specify due dates and deadlines.
6. Standards should be written.
7. Standards can be altered. Evaluate standards frequently and make appropriate changes to coincide with changes in the workplace.

The most important outcome of a performance planning session is that both participants know what is expected. If and when questions arise, both parties can consult the "plan" for clarification. The possibility of misunderstanding will be significantly reduced. Furthermore, employees who are directly involved in performance planning are more likely to be committed to making it work.

Here is a brief checklist for performance planning:

1. Write your plans.
2. Involve your employees in all planning stages.
3. Consider all aspects of a job.
4. Determine priorities.
5. Set performance standards that are specific, measurable, realistic, and challenging.

6. Be sure that the employee understands and accepts the sequence of activities required to fulfill each performance standard.
7. Set goals that relate directly to the employee's development needs.

Documenting performance

Another activity critical to the success of performance management is the collection of accurate and specific information about job behavior. Data gathering begins as soon as performance standards have been established and discussed. If you rely solely on memory to evaluate performance, the chances that your appraisal will be unbiased and accurate are minimal because few people have total recall and what they may remember of recent events may not reflect the total performance.

Although documenting workplace behaviors may seem to be a complicated task, record keeping can be simplified by using a file folder system (one file per employee) or a confidential computer record. On-the-job behaviors known as "critical incidents" can be recorded on single sheets of paper. Memory aids such as a notebook or 3 × 5 inch index cards are useful in gathering performance data on the spot. Your notes can consist of brief phrases jotted down in longhand, but they should contain at least enough information to enable you to recall the details of the event later. Significant events, whether favorable or unfavorable, should be brought to the employee's attention at the time they occur and can be used later as concrete examples of the employee's work. You can compile a comprehensive performance record by using these sources:

1. Performance data such as safety records, deadline records, quality of work samples, and absenteeism records
2. Direct observations of performance (i.e., "critical incidents")
3. Records of commendation
4. Disciplinary action reports
5. Notes taken from previous discussions related to work performance
6. Comments of other employees who have had direct contact with the employee on the job. (To ensure that such information is as objective as possible, try to find out exactly what kind of work was performed or observed and how that person would evaluate your employee's performance.)
7. Special activities performed which are outside the usual work requirements.

A performance record if it is to be used as a basis for a fair and accurate appraisal must include as many sources as possible. By gathering information as incidents occur, the observer is able to describe specific events, patterns of behavior, and other occurrences in detail. Thus vague impressions or "gut feelings" can be eliminated from the list of sources for a performance review. Concrete records of performance provide both continuous on-the-job feedback and an ongoing assessment that can be reviewed periodically by manager and employee.

You can ask employees to participate in the documentation by encouraging them to keep daily records of their work-related activities. Employees who are able to discuss their work in detail can take an active role in their own performance management. Here are two suggestions for employee participation:

1. Record each day's activities in a journal or a log. Be brief and concise. Use phrases. Quantify activities whenever possible (for example, "Spent half a day training two new employees to use emergency road service system"). Be sure to enter activities daily. Make entries a part of each day's routine.

2. Keep a file with examples of on-the-job activities such as reports, notes from meetings attended, materials produced, letters of commendation, training received, and extra work projects.

Planning periodic meetings to evaluate progress

Formal performance appraisal interviews tend to be annually conducted. Current research indicates, however, that one-time appraisals can be so stressful that they create more problems than may be solved. A single review session has several disadvantages: (1) employees may be surprised and unprepared for a negative review, (2) the interview usually attempts to cover too much in a single session, (3) a single interview may be ineffective for those employees with problems because significant change in employee behavior generally takes place over time, and (4) the overall performance rating may be unfair if recent behavior rather than total performance is used for the evaluation.[2] Continuous feedback is important to the success of this system. Employees deserve to know how well or poorly they are performing. Effective feedback should be provided regularly, appropriately, and constructively. Successful managers use feedback to motivate, counsel, and coach employees and to enhance their performance through knowledge and understanding of their individual needs.

The formal interview should be the culmination of a year-long performance management process. A series of meetings should be held *prior* to the formal review of an employee's performance. The first meeting should consist of a performance planning session at which the supervisor and employee agree on specific performance requirements, identify what is needed for achievement, and set goals for implementation. The planning period is followed by several formal or informal "progress" review sessions, which are augmented by ongoing documentation from both the supervisor and employee.

Most human resources experts agree that discussions concerning performance improvement, training, or career development should not be part of the formal appraisal interview.[3] In identifying the appraisal interview as the means of evaluating past performance, the manager takes on the role of critic and judge. When discussing development, the manager acts as a counselor or coach. Both roles are significant components of performance management, but combining the two makes it more difficult for managers to develop either role fully. One solution is to deal with performance development continuously. Any necessary coaching or counseling is thus performed *before* the formal appraisal interview. Another possibility is to set aside time for an in-depth counseling session to discuss plans for improving performance *after* the formal interview.[4]

If your current appraisal system mandates a year-end formal interview, you can still design a review schedule that will alleviate at least a few of the worst features of the one-time interview. here are some tips on how to adjust your schedule:

1. Know your employees. Consider what you already know about them and the nature of their work, then decide how often to schedule performance reviews.
2. Analyze your own needs carefully. Performance management of your staff must be balanced against your other responsibilities. Think of ways to evaluate work performance informally. Establishing a comfortable working relationship over a long period will ensure that both parties know what to expect at appraisal time.
3. Be as creative as possible. You may decide to meet weekly, quarterly, or semiannually, or you may want to schedule interviews at the end of a major project, when performance seems to have declined or accelerated, before a person is transferred or promoted, or when new duties are assigned.

Providing feedback

If you want to tell employees "how they're doing" you must know exactly what they are doing, and when and how they are doing it. The more you observe individual employee performance, the more you'll understand how to supervise each person. Obviously, some people need more help in performing work than others. In most cases, you can delegate tasks with the confidence that the employees will check back with you when they need guidance. Others may require daily or weekly contact. Individual differences, in fact, dictate the extent to which a manager must check on work. The important point is that performance management cannot be effective unless both parties know that performance expectations are being met satisfactorily through periodic feedback. Here are some guidelines for providing feedback:

1. Tell the employee immediately when something positive or negative occurs.
2. Explain positive and negative feedback carefully so that it is fully understood.
3. Show respect for the employee. Listen carefully to an employee's explanation. Indicate that you understand the employee's point of view.
4. Make sure that feedback is factual and accurate.[5]

Reciprocal feedback

An employee should feel comfortable about discussing day-to-day performance problems with you. One way to establish rapport is to encourage reciprocal feedback. If, during informal review sessions, you try to learn how *you* are doing as a manager, you are more likely to establish an effective working relationship since you are open to suggestions. Your genuine concern about achievement and productivity in your own performance can become an incentive for increased employee productivity. In addition, by obtaining as much information from as many sources as possible, you will promote rather than hold up your employee's development.

Coaching and counseling

Two communication techniques, coaching and counseling, are extremely helpful in performance management.[6] Of these two, coaching may be the more effective. Once performance standards have been established, both manager and employee should be operating under identical assumptions and expectations about the work being done. The manager is now in the position to act as coach while observing day-to-day performance, giving positive or negative feedback, and holding informal meetings to discuss progress. By encouraging your employees to do their jobs to the best of their ability, you reinforce good performance and create a positive work environment. The key to successful coaching is to let employees know that you have confidence in them, that you are paying attention to individual performance, and that their contribution to the entire "team" effort is essential.

Effective coaching includes the following strategies:

1. Get to know each employee. Develop a strong one-to-one relationship. Be accessible.

2. Encourage and praise good performance. Use positive reinforcement to support your employees.
3. Criticize whenever the situation warrants, but use tact and restraint. Discuss the problem, not the person. Take the time to learn how each employee reacts to criticism and act accordingly.
4. Be consistent. Communicate your expectations and follow through.
5. Be an attentive listener. Show your interest with relevant questions, eye contact, body language and tone of voice.

Counseling is an important communication technique at your disposal particularly when you spot a problem affecting performance adversely but which may not be work-related. Unlike coaching which involves directing the employee's performance, counseling is an interactive approach. You help identify a problem, look at solutions, and work with the employee to find the right solution. Counseling means helping the employee to manage his or her own problems. Problems, whether they exist in the workplace or outside, affect the productivity of everyone. As a manager, it is your responsibility to prevent problems from damaging individual and team efforts. You can do this by taking a genuine interest in your employees. Let them know that you value them not only as workers but also as individuals. Encourage them to discuss concerns so that time and effort are not wasted on needless worry. You should help them to arrive at problem-solving decisions without expressing an opinion about either the person or the decision. If the employee requests outside assistance, you can explore community resources for appropriate referrals.

1. John Bernardin and Richard W. Beatty, *Performance Appraisal: Assessing Human Behavior at Work* (Boston, Mass.: Kent Publishing Co., 1984), 343.
2. Richard I. Henderson, *Performance Appraisal* (Reston, Va.: Reston Publishing Co., 1984), 48.
3. H. Kent Baker, "Two Goals in Every Performance Appraisal" *Personnel Journal* (September 1984): 74–78.
4. Ibid.
5. Ervin Rausch, *Win-Win Performance Management/Appraisal* (New York: John Wiley & Sons, 1985), 45–46.
6. For a concise discussion of coaching and counseling, see John F. Azzaretto, "Coaching and Counseling," in *Effective Supervisory Practices Training Package* (Washington, DC: International City Management Association, 1984), 125–38.

Creating a Performance Management System

Craig Eric Schneier,
Richard W. Beatty, and Lloyd S. Baird

Managers frequently complain about the time and effort required to write performance objectives, complete appraisal forms, document performance problems, and hold formal performance feedback sessions. Why shouldn't they complain? After all, do managers get promoted because they complete subordinates' appraisal forms on time? They realize they get promoted because they manage subordinates' performance effectively and achieve desired results. Few managers disagree with this basic notion—their job is to manage the performance of their subordinates. They admit that they hold performance expectations for their subordinates, monitor performance, let subordinates know when they have erred, form overall evaluations of each subordinate, and recommend that various actions be taken as a result of their evaluations. In short, they, with varying degrees of skill, perform key performance appraisal tasks and activities routinely as they carry out their responsibilities.

It is the view that performance appraisal lies outside of these activities that renders it less than useful to managers. Those activities managers already see as legitimate can be termed performance management. By providing managers with a performance management perspective, by detailing a set of sequential performance management activities, and by building their performance management skills, we have been able to show that performance appraisal is integral to their jobs. This has paved the way for successful performance appraisal systems.

Rather than attempt to design and implement an appraisal system (merely a form and the policies governing its use), we imple-

Reprinted with permission of the authors from the May 1986 issue of *Training and Development Journal.*

Figure 1. Sample skills and related knowledge required for performance management.

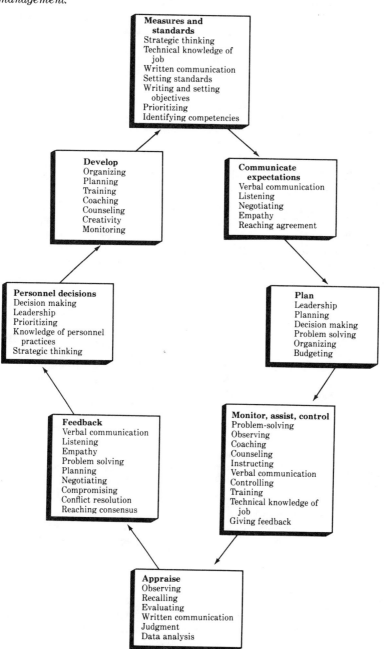

Measures and standards
Strategic thinking
Technical knowledge of job
Written communication
Setting standards
Writing and setting objectives
Prioritizing
Identifying competencies

Develop
Organizing
Planning
Training
Coaching
Counseling
Creativity
Monitoring

Communicate expectations
Verbal communication
Listening
Negotiating
Empathy
Reaching agreement

Personnel decisions
Decision making
Leadership
Prioritizing
Knowledge of personnel practices
Strategic thinking

Plan
Leadership
Planning
Decision making
Problem solving
Organizing
Budgeting

Feedback
Verbal communication
Listening
Empathy
Problem solving
Planning
Negotiating
Compromising
Conflict resolution
Reaching consensus

Monitor, assist, control
Problem-solving
Observing
Coaching
Counseling
Instructing
Verbal communication
Controlling
Training
Technical knowledge of job
Giving feedback

Appraise
Observing
Recalling
Evaluating
Written communication
Judgment
Data analysis

ment systems by helping managers effectively manage performance. We have emphasized the performance management skills and related knowledge required of managers (see Figure 1). Training programs can be designed efficiently to teach skills once a needs assessment has been conducted. Since several skills overlap, and the cycle is seen as a legitimate part of their job by most managers, performance management training usually is received well. Activities such as video-based behavior modeling, cases, role-plays, questionnaires, lectures, and group projects all help. Most importantly, the skills easily transfer to job performance because they are essentially general managerial skills. The eight-step performance management cycle follows.

Choose performance appraisal measures and standards

Those aspects of job performance that have an impact on success, differentiate between successful and unsuccessful performers, and are at least partially within the control of the person being rated should be identified as performance measures. Since most jobs are multidimensional, multiple measures will be chosen. Certainly, measures may be weighted differentially, depending on contribution to overall performance. A thorough, systematic job analysis and an accurate, concise position description are an excellent basis for determining performance measures.[1]

Job analyses and position descriptions provide a view of the job by detailing duties, responsibilities, and tasks. The appraisal measures may include all or some of these. The crucial question asks what is important to evaluate from the descriptive set of duties. If each task a job incumbent performs is to be evaluated, there must be a method for measuring performance on each. Typically, only a subset of tasks, or a series of tasks grouped together, warrants inclusion in the appraisal system.

The development of performance standards—methods for making judgments about performance—becomes far less complex and problematic when viewed from the manager's perspective. A manager is concerned with three possible measures: what people achieve, what people do, and what people "are." They translate, respectively, into assessing results, assessing behaviors, and assessing personal characteristics. Each dictates a specific type of appraisal format, discussed briefly below:

Behavior-based systems   Appraisal measures can be defined by specific, job-related behaviors, as in behaviorally anchored rating scales (see Figure 2). These performance appraisal formats present specific behavioral examples for each performance level.[2] They and related behaviorally based systems are useful because they detail

Figure 2. A behaviorally anchored rating scale (BARS).

Job title: Division Audit Manager
Job dimension: Conducting Meetings and Briefings

Unacceptable

Fails to prepare for briefings or meetings and to recognize the status and needs of the audience.

Fails to convey that division made reasonable efforts to investigate or resolve an issue by not being able to link audit scope and methodology to objective.

Has extreme difficulty in responding to basic questions on status of audit assignment.

Creates hostile environment by being critical of corporate participants during meetings.

Borderline

Displays limited preparedness for meetings with corporate staffs.

Generally has difficulty in determining when and what visual aids would be beneficial for a meeting.

Has difficulty discussing audit assignment scope, methodology, objectives and expected results in a clear, concise manner. Responses to questions in briefings are verbose and on some occasions inaccurate.

Fully Successful

Can conduct entire briefing or meeting with corporate staffs. Adequately prepared and presents information in a clear, concise manner, devoid of ambiguity.

Responses to questions are direct. Displays some awareness of corporate participants' understanding of the information and more often than not adjusts the detail of information presented accordingly.

Superior

Controls the tempo of meetings by awareness of time constraints and level of understanding by the corporate audience.

Rarely is nonresponsive to questions concerning the audit/project assignment.

Concludes meetings with summary of information presented and agreements reached.

Uses concise visual aids.

Always has written agenda and manages time to end when planned.

Exceptional

Visual aids are conducive to effective presentation of information and are creative, as well as accurate and concise.

Anticipates questions which may be asked on the subject topic of the meeting or on related topics and responds in a clear, concise manner.

Shows unusual ability to sense how the meeting is going and adjusts tempo and sequence accordingly. Always is sure that mutual agreements exist among the participants on any additional or future work to be done prior to concluding meeting.

Receives letters of appreciation and praise and/or receives positive feedback in briefing or meeting.

Figure 3. Sample managerial competencies. *

Concern for cost-effectiveness
Advocate of organization mission
Sense of priorities
Cooperates as a member of the management team
Understanding of groups
Creative thinking skill
Knowledge of organization business strategies
Knowledge of customer base
Expressive communication skill
Risk taker
Concern with impact
Strategic thinking
Tolerance for ambiguity
Supportive managerial style

*Definitions and behavioral illustrations are omitted.

what is required to perform effectively and reduce bias in ratings. Just as important, they help communicate a manager's performance expectations to subordinates. Competencies can be defined behaviorally, as can specific job duties.

Competency-based systems   Measures can also be built around competencies—knowledge, skills, abilities, motivation and other personal characteristics that lead to high performance. These must be characteristics (e.g., cooperation, setting priorities, risk-taking) that distinguish between effective and ineffective performers.[3] They must also be well defined in behavioral terms in order to reduce subjectivity in their application. Competency-based performance appraisal systems recognize the importance of how an individual's characteristics influence results obtained. They capture the organization culture by describing "what it takes to make it" and thus should be developed in each specific organization in which they will be used. (A sample set of competencies that we developed for organizations to enhance the realism and utility of their performance appraisal systems appear in Figure 3.)

The choice of measures, as well as the methods of measuring chosen and the resulting performance appraisal format, depend on the nature and level of the job in question, the uses intended for the system, and various unique job context characteristics. No one technique applies universally and combination systems often are useful. For example, managers could be evaluated by using a set of objectives to measure outputs or results achieved and with competencies, containing behavioral examples for different performance levels, to measure the process of managing.

Communicate performance expectations

Once appraisal measures have been determined and performance expectations defined for each level of performance, these expectations must be communicated to those being rated. Negotiation and participation are crucial. Superiors must follow up to be sure expectations are understood.

Plan for performance

Here, the manager helps subordinates develop strategies and plans to meet performance expectations and secure required resources. Action plans are necessary, as are budgets and time schedules. The impact of goal attainment on other units must be considered. Critical relationships between activities must be specified and alternative strategies developed before an effective plan can be implemented. The manager secures necessary resources (information, money, people, technology) to facilitate high performance by clearing a path to goal attainment.

Monitor, assist, and control performance

A crucial distinction between performance appraisal and performance management is that the former is often seen by managers merely as a once- or twice-a-year activity. While designers of performance appraisal systems admonish managers to view them as a continual process, a specific set of ongoing activities is not well articulated for managers. Managers do agree that they *manage* performance each day, all year long, but perhaps only *appraise* performance annually. Hence, this step is a key part of performance management. Here, the manager monitors performance and provides ongoing feedback, both positive and negative. One popular method is "Management by wandering around," which recognizes that managers need to be away from their desks, observing performance, comparing it to expectations, and intervening in the ongoing process using behavior-based language to improve performance. Problem-solving, coaching, counseling, developing, and removing obstacles to success may all be required during a formal interim review. Performance must also be controlled and corrective action taken, as necessary. Managers must be skilled at diagnosing causes of performance problems and at improving performance.

Appraise performance

This is the step typically thought of as performance appraisal. Performance observations are recalled and judgments are made, comparing what is recalled to the rater's interpretation of the standards set in the first step. Complexities of processing information and making judgments are particularly relevant in this step of the performance management cycle. Several strategies are helpful for assisting raters in their job. First, concrete, perhaps behaviorally based performance measures are useful. Second, expectations should be communicated to ratees, thus reducing the potential for subsequent disagreements. Third, raters should document performance, both positive and negative, to assist them in recall and in basing their judgments on a representative sample of performance. Finally, rater training, building both sensitivity to judgment problems and skill in overcoming them through practice, can be very useful.

Many rater training programs emphasize how to complete forms or address possible rating errors such as "leniency" or "halo." Sensitization to such problems is not sufficient. Effective programs should build raters' skills in communication, coaching, planning, listening, negotiating, observing, problem solving, and in those skills related to various phases of the performance management cycle. Rather than merely disseminating information to raters, workshops utilizing modeling and practice can facilitate skill-building.[4,5]

Provide performance feedback

While the performance management cycle calls for continuous feedback, a formal feedback session should be held subsequent to the appraisal. Here, superiors provide a rationale for their evaluation and allow ratees to participate in the discussion. In providing feedback, raters must distinguish between inferences or conclusions about behavior and behavior itself. The most useful feedback contains facts about behavior, not conclusions or inferences (see Figure 4). Relying on inference leads to defensiveness. Energy is wasted on denying allegations and arguing about judgments, as opposed to solving performance problems. Feedback also should be specific and should not overemphasize the negative.

In order to increase the probability that problems will be addressed, managers must listen without evaluating. They must help set a positive, open tone. A time and place free of interruptions are required. A detailed plan should be developed indicating specific actions to be taken by the individual, the superior, and the organization, as well as dates for each action.

The performance review discussion is also an opportunity to use results of previous steps in the performance management cycle and to demonstrate the ongoing nature of its activities. Documenting past performance, identifying specific measures, communicating performance expectations, and using results of both the interim review and the final appraisal are relevant at this step.

Using performance results for decision making

Subsequent to a final rating and performance review session, various decisions can be made, based on the appraisal results. Decisions

Figure 4. Inferential and behavioral performance feedback.

Inferential feedback	Behavioral feedback
Tells about how other person feels; makes "you" statements	Tells about the event
Cannot be observed or verified	Can be observed and verified
Agreement is difficult	Makes agreement easier
Uses the verbs "to be," "to know"	Uses action verbs
Uses absolutes	Differentiates clearly
General/abstract	Concrete/specific; doesn't use adverbs
Value judgment	Free of values
Attributes causes or motives	Not locked into attributing causes or motives
Examples	**Examples**
You don't care....	The report contained a very concise, useful conclusion
You don't know....	Your language with the client was vague
You don't take into consideration....	Six absences in two months is not acceptable
You need to be more conscientious	The contract omitted a vital section
You should know these things	The data analysis was inaccurate according to my figures
Good work	I observed you interrupting that subordinate
You are never here when I need you	
You always come late when we have meetings	
Don't say	**Say ...**
"You're rude and tactless with other employees."	"You left Rosena very hurt and angry when you told her that she was not dressed well enough to attend the luncheon meeting and not bright enough to participate."
"The work you turn in contains too many stupid errors."	"The computer programmers are having difficulty in processing your work because of coding mistakes."
"You really botched the the semiconductor contract."	"We had a lot of trouble processing the semiconductor contract because forms were incomplete."

Source: S. O'Connell, *Manager As Communicator* (Harper & Row, 1981).

related to promotion, demotion, or termination; to allocation of monetary and other types of incentives and awards; and to job assignment are examples. In an integrated, interdependent set of HRD activities and programs, ouputs of the performance management system become inputs for other systems.

For example, the rating itself becomes the rationale for awarding merit increases. The control and monitoring process identifies performance problems that influence training program design efforts. Developmental discussions are used to make human resource plans and forecasts, and are the data base for career development programs and activities. Appraisal measure—detailing performance expectations of a position—are naturally used as selection and promotion criteria.

To ensure success, the results of the appraisal process must be used to affect people's jobs, careers, and rewards. In addition, basing such decisions on performance management results allows the process to become integrated into overall management of the organization and for the results to appear.

Developing performance

The last step in the ongoing performance management cycle is development of performance. The supervisor, individual, and organization each have responsibilities to develop and improve performance. Here HRD professionals and specialists have a critical role. The organization might provide funds for furthering formal education or offer in-house training and self-assessment. The supervisor might agree to coach a subordinate more frequently or provide an opportunity to enhance job responsibilities. The individual might plan to read current technical information, attend professional society meetings, or learn a new skill. Subsequent to the performance feedback session, a structured individual development plan is useful. It can pinpoint what is required in order to assure that performance develops over time.

The essentials of implementing a performance management system include: setting clear project objectives, obtaining commitment from top management and users, overcoming resistance to change, allowing for participation of users in design phases, conducting pilot testing, building early successes, and continually redesigning and revising. But the system begins with the premise that performance management is not an additional function or responsibility of managers designed by HRD or personnel staff, but a more systematic and effective system for managing performance. This system views management and recognizes the organizational culture in the following ways:

As a solution to managerial problems   Implementation of performance management begins with an analysis of managers' performance management problems and their performance management skill levels. Among these problems might be dealing with poor performance; communicating realistic performance expectations; defending promotion decisions; or planning, scheduling, and delegating work. Performance management does not begin with the HRD staff's problems, which might include an "invalid" appraisal system, appraisal forms not completed, or lack of data on organization-wide deficiencies required to defend a training program. Addressing managers' problems leads to implementing a viable managerial tool (as well as a solution to the HRD staff problems).

As a tool to capture and influence an organization's culture   Much has been written about the importance of organization culture in improving performance and productivity. The performance management system can help to identify and define salient aspects of the culture by specifying behaviors required for success and competencies necessary to succeed in a given organization, unit, group, or position. Managers especially appreciate a system that has the ring of truth and recognizes valued characteristics. When an appraisal form contains terms like "work quality" or "work quantity," but promotion decisions really hinge on such terms as "is a team player," "can take the heat," and "is tactful," the formal system loses credibility.

System implementation must be preceded by a dialogue about organization strategy, mission, and objectives. Strategic-level decisions include what personal characteristics are required for long-term survival, how excellent performance will be recognized, how potential will be identified, how the system will be used in key decisions, and how the HRD function will be organized to facilitate performance management.[6,7]

Putting staff specialists in the role of facilitator, consultant, and technical expert   Ownership lies with the users, not staff. Staff does not play an "enforcer" role, ultimately leading to conflict with line managers, but gains visibility, legitimacy, and power from its ability to help managers solve real problems with tools that recognize realities of managers' work styles and work environments.

To implement performance management, a group of managers with performance-related problems is shown the basic model and its rationale. They develop, with HRD staff assistance, performance measures, expectations or standards, action plans, and documentation devices. Supporting programs for orientation and training (skill-building) are designed. Policies governing administration, timing, and use of data are set in advance and are enforced. Relationships of data to other human resource systems and programs are made explicit. Managers begin to use performance management with staff assistance, if required. Revisions are made to enhance utility and relevance for various job settings, but certain overall standards are maintained.

Implementing, complying legally, and validating the system   While performance management is a system of managerial activities—not a set of forms to complete—any documentation of performance, any evaluations, and any decisions made using appraisal data must be assessed as to legal compliance. Guidelines have been offered to designers of appraisal systems which assist in meeting legal requirements.[8] Among these are the following:

1. Written instructions on forms
2. Appraisal measures derived through job analysis
3. Performance standards based on work actually performed
4. An absence of "adverse impact" on "protected groups" as a result of decisions based on appraisals
5. User orientation and training programs
6. Appeal and review provisions
7. No exclusive reliance on "subjective" evaluations of supervisors
8. Ample opportunity for raters to observe ratees

While methods for assessing various validity strategies are available, the system generates valid personnel decisions. It relies on job-related criteria and standards based on job analyses. It emphasizes training of users and communication of performance expectations. And, it allows for review and appeal of rating, forces actual rater observation, and recommends use of performance-contingent rewards.

1. Beatty, R.W., & Schneier, C.E. (1981). *Personnel administration: An experiential/skill-building approach.* 2nd ed. Addison-Wesley.
2. Schneier, C.E., & Beatty, R.W. (August 1979). Developing behaviorally-anchored rating scales. *The Personnel Administrator,* 24(8), 65-78.
3. Boyatziz, R.E. (1982). *The competent manager.* Wiley.
4. Sashkin, M. (1981). *Assessing performance appraisal.* University Associates.
5. Baird, L., Schneier, C.E., and Laird, D., *The training and development sourcebook* (1984). Human Resource Development Press.
6. Fombrun, C.J., et al. (1984). *Strategic human resource management.* Wiley.
7. Baird, L.S. (1985). *Performance management.* Wiley.
8. Schneier, C.E., & Beatty, R.W. (1984). Designing a legally defensible performance appraisal system. In M. Cohen and R. Golembiewski (eds.), *Public personnel update.* Marcel Dekker.

Making Merit Pay Work

Most organizations reward outstanding performers with a pay increase. In theory, merit pay is a sound performance reward; increased pay reinforces excellent work activity and motivates employees to do their best. Furthermore, merit pay is distributed according to "performance," as defined by the performance appraisal system.

In practice, however, many merit pay systems fail to consistently fulfill their mission of rewarding superior performance. Even worse, some merit pay schemes actually hinder solid work performance by causing motivated, enthusiastic employees to become frustrated and disenchanted.

Why does the theoretically sound merit pay approach fail so often in real work situations? Too often, the fault lies with the appraisal system upon which merit pay distribution is based.

This article will focus on the key role played by the performance appraisal system in making merit pay work. We will begin by examining some of the most common problems with merit pay administration. Next, we will discuss obstacles to effective evaluation of employee performance. Finally, we will outline effective methods for detecting, counteracting, and preventing the performance appraisal flaws that work against effective merit pay.

Problems with merit pay administration

The three main problems with merit pay administration are (1) that pay is perceived as being unrelated to job performance; (2) that secrecy of pay is related to perceived inequity; and (3) that the size of the merit increase has little impact on performance.

Pay and performance   Managers are often unhappy with their wage system because they do not see the relationship between level of work effort and level of earnings. There are several reasons for this perception; one of the most common is that so much time elapses between performance and reward that the employee (as well as the manager) loses sight of the relationship. Without this link, reinforcement will be ineffective and could possibly undermine more intrinsic types of motivation, such as doing a good job or feeling a sense of accomplishment when work is well done.

The goals or objectives that the employee is supposed to accomplish are often unclear, nonspecific, or unrealistic. Because goals are not developed properly in many cases, many managers think goal attainment has little bearing on merit increase.

Many times, the merit increase is based on other factors than performance, further obscuring the relationship between performance and pay. These factors include length of service, the manager's perception of future potential, or a perceived need to "catch up" where one employee's pay is low compared with that of others in the group. Often, these and other administrative concerns or traditions override the more fundamental relationship of merit pay to outstanding job performance.

Pay and secrecy   Pay secrecy often flourishes when performance appraisals are not linked to realistic objectives and standards. Without clear criteria for making performance decisions, managers have a difficult time mustering convincing arguments to support their salary decisions. To compound the lack of criteria for decision making, managers in many companies lack an accurate picture of what other managers above them and below them are earning. Such lack of communication adds to the difficulty of making salary decisions.

Secrecy of merit pay also causes problems with employees. Pay secrecy has been cited as a major source of perceptions of inequity. Edward E. Lawler III points out that employees overestimate the pay of their peers and underestimate the pay of their bosses;[1] both of these perceptions damage pay-for-performance expectancy.

Size of increase   Surveys have indicated that most raises are too small to be effective. For example, a survey of 2,867 companies conducted by *The Wall Street Journal* in 1979 found that salary increases were too low to motivate employees. Pay can be motivating if the increase is large enough in relation to an individual's income to result in a significant change in financial condition. In order to be effective, such an increase would have to be on the order of 20% to 30%.

Fixed budgets

While the concept of rewarding outstanding performers with a pay increase seems straightforward and logical, in practice it is very difficult to implement properly. In fact, organizations typically do not have enough money to pay for performance; instead, departments are allotted a fixed percentage increase in their salary budgets, which forces the manager to limit the amount of raises he or she can allow.

Pay, therefore, is determined not by performance but by the amount of money allocated in the year's salary pool. An individual's salary increase usually is based on the manager's creativity in "backing into" performance ratings to make the numbers match up. Often these decisions are arbitrary or subjective, characteristics that enrage and often demoralize the workers affected.

Why performance appraisals fail

Performance appraisal is commonly linked to merit pay. It serves to identify and rate the performance of employees; based on this rating, a certain amount of merit pay is allotted to that individual. To be effective, a performance appraisal system must be perceived by the manager as a practical managerial tool; in addition, employees must believe that it is fair and that it accurately rates their performance. There are several reasons why performance appraisal systems often do not meet these criteria.

An annual event   Most employees find out about their performance once a year when the performance appraisal form is filled out. The filling out of the form is usually a response to extreme pressure by the personnel department so that the employee can receive his or her yearly salary increase. The appraisal is typically an undesirable task because the forms often do not describe what the employee's duties really are, which causes the employee to ask a lot of questions that the manager can't answer.

Poorly defined performance standards   Many appraisal systems have an elaborate rating format with four or five standards or levels of performance. The system often has a plus (+) and a minus (−) attached to each standard. The result is eight to ten performance categories that are designed to "let people know where they stand."

However, the differences among these performance categories are hardly ever stated. In fact, the difference between a "satisfactory" and a "satisfactory plus" cannot be operationally defined in most appraisal systems. It is this illusion of precise ranking—without substantiation—that limits the system's effectiveness.

While this type of system is susceptible to individual rater bias, it also forces a manager to spend valuable time playing the "rating game." Merit plans are based on the assumption that managers can make valid distinctions between good and poor levels of performance. Most evaluations, however, are subjective and consist of a summary score from a generalized evaluation form.

Need to maintain equity   Since the criteria for outstanding and even average performance are unclear, the manager must try to give ratings that do not appear to favor any one employee over the others. Maintaining equity within the work unit becomes essential because in most cases the manager cannot accurately justify his or her decisions if employees demand to know how the performance ratings were determined.

Forced ranking   Performance ratings and the salary increases tied to them are often distributed along a normal curve or some other fixed formula of distribution. Forced ranking systems allow only a certain number of employees in a given work unit to be rated in any particular category. For example, one Fortune 500 company allowed only 20% of the employees of any work group to be rated as outstanding.

These types of systems run contrary to the very purpose of management. Managers are charged with helping all their workers become excellent performers; however, the system forces managers to label many outstanding or potentially superior employees as "average" in order to justify merit ratings, thereby losing these employees' trust and confidence in the process.

Boss-centered   In practice, this reminds the employee very clearly that he or she is dependent on the supervisor for rewards. If that supervisor is a mediocre or poor manager, the trust levels between manager and employee can deteriorate rapidly. Thus the system undermines less competent managers rather than supporting them.

Conflicting goals   Most organizations are structured by functional units (e.g., marketing, manufacturing, R&D, and finance). These departments and the work units within them are in turn evaluated for functionally oriented objectives. Appraisal systems hold managers accountable for achieving their work units' objectives. If there are conflicts in goals and objectives between work units and/or functional units, these systems will solidify such conflicts rather than promote organizational functioning.

Goals are barriers   How do goals become barriers to organizational performance? Performance objectives are set by managers to meet their goals—goals that may or may not be in the best interests of the organization. For example, manufacturing objectives often fail to reinforce marketing objectives. Instead, functional units regularly and unknowingly work against themselves, inhibiting teamwork and blocking organizational integration.

Individuals caught in this system focus on the needs of their boss, who controls and distributes the rewards, not on the needs of the organization or the customer. An employee's bonus, raise, and family security are dependent on meeting the boss's objectives, not the company's or customer's objectives.

Goals can enhance mediocrity   The fear of being punished or even fired for not meeting the boss's objectives limits risk taking and innovation on the part of most employees. Because they understand how the system works, employees negotiate for easily attainable goals in order to reduce their liability and increase their chances of goal attainment. Such a goal-setting process often results in the setting of mediocre rather than ambitious goals; this dulls the competitive edge companies are trying to maintain and improve.

Short-term vision   This type of objective setting encourages employees to focus on short-term accomplishments rather than on the organization's long-term success. It also promotes competition for the few high ratings allowed by the forced-ranking system. Employees competing for short-term gains inhibit cooperation and teamwork between all employees, both those within the work unit and those between work units.

System inflexibility   Jobs are dynamic; they change frequently during the course of the year because of a variety of unpredictable circumstances. On the other hand, most performance appraisal systems are static; their format is usually determined months before it is used. As job responsibilities and environments change, the performance appraisal form may become obsolete before it is even used.

Because many appraisal forms have fixed categories, they cannot be adjusted to fit changes in worker competence. Workers' performance levels change over time, possibly because of experience or training, thus rendering previously set standards of performance inappropriate or unfair.

Managers and employees experience many of these problems with performance appraisal systems. It is no wonder that many individuals in both camps are confused and frustrated and that many

Exhibit 1. Performance management cycle.

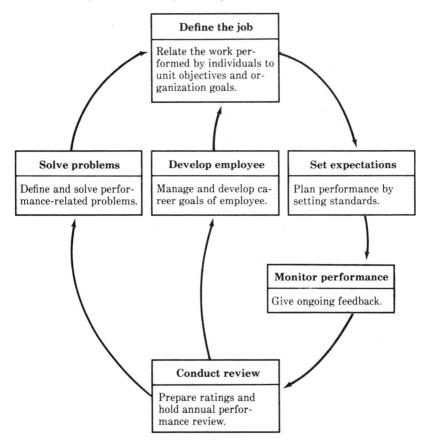

see little practical value in their appraisal systems. While no system is perfect, there are several ways to enhance a system's effectiveness.

The solution: performance management

To be effective, performance appraisal must be used in a much different way. Performance appraisal should not be used merely to complete a form once a year so that employees can get a raise; it must be transformed into performance *management,* a *process* of managing people every day.

Using performance management   In contrast with the once-a-year task of performance appraisal, performance management is an ongoing process. It is more than merely filling out a form; the performance management process can be seen as a cycle. (See Exhibit 1.) The cycle is a sequential set of managerial tasks and responsibilities that jointly define day-to-day activities.

The cycle begins with the definition of the most important job duties and outcomes of a particular position. The key question is, "What needs to be accomplished?" These accomplishments can include general job duties, specific work outcomes, work behaviors that define success at the job, or personal characteristics.

Once objectives have been defined with the employee, specific performance standards must be clearly communicated to him or her so that performance expectations are understood. Standards should be established with the aid of employee input, the extent of which depends on the employee's experience, the complexities of the job, the trust level between the manager and the employee, and the level of understanding of the work unit.

Once objectives and standards have been established, the manager monitors the employee's performance. Here the manager uses coaching and communication skills to direct employees toward success. Performance problems are identified and resolved at this stage; the manager may also need to adjust, add, or delete certain objectives to accurately respond to changing work-unit conditions.

In addition, there should be one or several interim appraisals to let the employee know how he or she is performing and to give honest and candid feedback. These interim appraisals will give each individual the opportunity to improve poor performance, to recognize and reinforce good performance, and to help ensure that there are no "surprises" at appraisal time.

At the time of the appraisal, the manager must rate the employee's performance on the basis of objectives and standards they have mutually agreed upon. Using concrete examples of work behavior, anecdotal records kept during the appraisal period, and interim appraisal results, the manager can give fair and equitable ratings to the employee.

In the formal appraisal interview, the manager should detail strengths and weaknesses, give concrete examples of performance, identify performance problems, and develop an action plan to help the employee be more successful on the job. Ratings should also be used to help determine promotions, raises, and future responsibilities and preferences that the employee may want to accomplish.

Integrating the organization Performance management also links together other organizational systems to improve continuity and focus throughout the organization. (See Exhibit 2.)

This organizational linkage is achieved by incorporating and developing objectives that reinforce and complement key organiza-

Exhibit 2. How performance management integrates the organization.

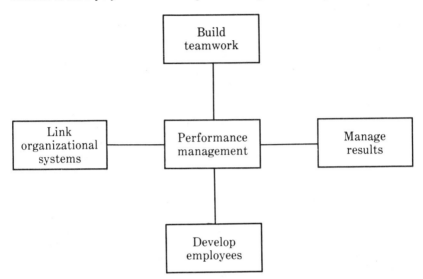

tional systems such as the corporate strategic plan, the quality improvement plan, succession planning, and others.

Developing objectives from other systems helps to integrate the organization and to ensure that all organizational levels are moving in the same direction. These types of objectives link important organizational goals across departments, reinforcing continuity and a common focus.

However, it may be difficult at some organizational levels to directly implement objectives from these systems into meaningful goals for individual employees. For example, a front-line supervisor may not be able to easily integrate the objectives of the corporate strategic plan into his or her work unit.

Finding the right objectives   When managers write objectives for their work units, how do they know these objectives are the right ones? Do their objectives promote interdepartmental cooperation and support the goals of the organization? The use of a technique called the *user approach* helps identify effective objectives. (See Exhibit 3.)

The user approach technique identifies objectives in relation to the work unit's customers. The manager identifies the users of the outputs of his or her work unit and then determines how these outputs can be changed to better meet user requirements.

In the user approach, the customers can be other units within the same department, other departments, or the buyers of the products and services themselves. Objectives that make products or services more effective for a work unit's users foster cooperation and organizational integration among work units, and begin to minimize conflicting and competing objectives. They also help employees understand how their jobs fit into the context of the larger organization.

The developmental needs of employees also determine where effective objectives should be identified. These objectives develop the employees' careers and stimulate creativity and entrepreneurship within an organization. They should focus on specific results or behaviors that will help employees be more successful in performing their job duties, enhance career opportunities within the organization, or promote innovation and creativity within their job responsibilities.

Making the system work   It is vitally important that managers and employees jointly set objectives. Recent studies by William Rabinowitz, Kenneth Falkenback, and Rosabeth Moss Kanter have concluded that workers want to know how they fit into the corporate picture, and want as well to participate in decisions that affect them. Employees will also be more committed to objectives and standards that they have helped develop.

Participative goal setting improves the chances of increasing productivity and quality since it gives employees a clearer understanding of what is expected of them. This clarification of expectations allows employees to monitor their own performance much more easily, thus improving the quality of their work effort.

Communicating with a common language   The joint planning of objectives establishes a common language about the work to be accom-

Exhibit 3. The user approach to identifying effective job objectives.

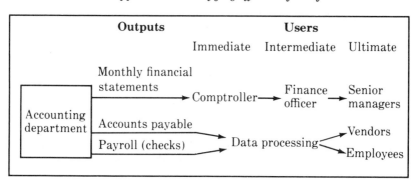

plished. This common language enables manager and employee to more easily discuss performance since they have both contributed to a common frame of reference. Facilitating discussion about work opens up communication on important work issues and reduces employee anxiety and defensiveness. Increased communication between manager and employee helps put the latter person "on the team" and increases trust and teamwork within the work unit.

Fostering flexibility   Participation in and open discussion of objectives and standards result in a flexible system that can be adapted to changes in job conditions. This adaptability makes the system more useful to managers in effectively managing the performance of their employees; it also more truly reflects the work the employee is doing. Performance management flexibility facilitates and reinforces communication and helps make the performance rating more meaningful and fair.

Integrating results with behavior   Managing performance is the process of observing, identifying, measuring, and developing work behavior in the organization. Most appraisal systems are either results-based or behavior-based; each of these systems has its advantages and disadvantages.

The results-based system focuses on what the employee produces or contributes to the work unit or organization. This method measures certain elements of productivity using a variety of quantitative, qualitative, and timeliness indicators. Such indicators are very applicable to task-oriented job positions within organizations; however, they become less useful with professional or creative job duties.

Behavior-based systems focus on *how* the employee should be performing his or her job duties; they provide specific examples of a range of successful and unacceptable employee behaviors as they relate to a specific job dimension. Behavior-based systems are excellent feedback mechanisms for employees, and they have been demonstrated to significantly improve job performance. However, behavior-based systems do not measure as many aspects of productivity as do results-based systems.

Some experts have argued that both types of systems should be integrated to guide and direct performance. These combined systems not only define short- and long-term goals for the individual in terms of *what* is expected; they also provide parameters in terms of *how* to attain those objectives. In this way an employee can be guided and evaluated on how to properly perform his or her job responsibilities. Such guidance and evaluation are particularly important when developing employees or building teams, since results may fall short of expectations through no fault of the employee.

How organizations do it

Many organizations have successful pay-for-performance systems because they have turned performance appraisal into performance management. Donald E. Peterson, chairman of the Ford Motor Company, feels that traditional systems are wasteful of human resources. Peterson is quoted as saying, "The waste results from excessive internal competition, not getting to the root causes of problems, and reinventing the wheel—to name a couple of situations where teamwork should pay dividends."[2]

As a result, Ford is experimenting with a system that rates the employee as working either within or outside of managerial expectations. Ford estimates that 90% to 95% of their employees meet expectations. These individuals do not receive "merit" increases in pay; instead, they share evenly the monies set aside for salary increases. Employees working below managerial expectations receive no pay increase; employees who are performing above managerial expectations receive a merit increase (in addition to the salary share given to employees who meet performance expectations).

A Western utility company is basing its pay increases on the achievement of its yearly objectives. If the objectives are achieved, all employees receiving an overall rating of satisfactory or above share evenly in the funds available for salary increases. Employees who are rated below satisfactory do not share in the salary increase for that year. This approach, like the one at Ford, focuses attention on teamwork and organizational integration rather than on individual achievement, regardless of the state of the organization.

Companies like 3M use other rewards to stimulate what E. L. Deci has called *intrinsic motivation*.[3] These companies offer employees a certain amount of resources and up to 15% of their time from the regular workweek to develop their own projects. These rewards are offered through departmental as well as through corporate funds. To receive these types of rewards, employees must have their projects approved by their department manager.

Employees who apply for rewards and are turned down can go around their department and receive resources through the Genesis Fund, a corporate controlled account, to further develop their ideas. Employees at 3M are also permitted in some instances to "bootleg" onto other projects to further their own professional interests and motivation.

Other companies also offer recognition for achievement. For example, IBM has the 100 Percent Club for salespeople who achieve their sales quotas. IBM also manages its salesforce so that 95% of its salespeople qualify for club membership. The Foxboro Company has the Golden Banana Award for outstanding contributions to the company, and 3M has the Carlton Society, the Golden Step Award, the Pathfinder Award, and other awards for a variety of accomplishments.

Other companies believe that motivation is best served when members of an organization participate in some of the decisions that directly affect them. These organizations feel that when workers participate meaningfully in the work situation, they will be constructive and support the activities of that organization. For example, workers in some companies are being rewarded for their participation in problem solving or quality teams through such gainsharing arrangements as the Scanlon Plan at Eggers Industries.

These ways of rewarding employees for innovative and constructive problem solving, as well as for solid job performance, are dependent on managers' knowing how to administer their system in a clear, understandable, and consistent manner. These skills do not come naturally; managers who are good at such skills practice them continually. Furthermore, companies generally invest training dollars in their managers, to ensure that they know how to effectively administer the company's performance management efforts.

1. Edward E. Lawler III, "Merit Pay: Fact or Fiction?" *Management Review*, April 1981.
2. W.W. Scherkenbach, "Performance Appraisal and Quality: Ford's New Philosophy," *Quality Progress*, April 1985.
3. E.L. Deci, "The Hidden Costs of Rewards," *Organizational Dynamics*, Winter 1976.

PART 4

Developing Performance Standards

Development of Performance Standards: A Practical Guide

Since its inception, the Denver Career Service Authority has been wrestling with how to improve its employee evaluation system and encourage better performance appraisal by supervisors. The Authority has changed its rating form repeatedly; amended its rules; and trained hundreds of supervisors in how to use it. But regardless of the form used, the emphasis of its rules, and the specific training given, the evaluation system fell short of helping workers know and meet the work expectations of supervisors. Consequently, it has not met the real goal of employee evaluation—assisting employees in becoming better workers.

In the late 1970s, the Career Service Training Section began reviewing the literature on performance evaluations, studying other systems, and reviewing different approaches to resolve the Authority's evaluation dilemma. What has developed is a training commitment to a format for developing performance standards for specific jobs. Many hours of work with individual supervisors from a variety of working agencies have been spent in assisting them in the development of tailor-made standards.

This article presents a broad training format for the development of performance standards. It has been expanded, modified, and tailored by operating agency supervisors to meet their specific needs. This system is voluntary and thus has not been used in all agencies or by all supervisors; but those that have chosen this management method have had success.

While this method is not a panacea for management, the experience in utilizing the system has produced many side benefits.

Reprinted with permission of the International Personnel Management Association from the Summer 1987 issue of *Public Personnel Management.*

Better communication between the supervisor and employees is assured as both are actively involved. Better work flow and organization can result because of the information generated during this process. Data related to work flow is easily picked up during the process. The time necessary to complete the process is paid back in higher morale, less time spent in preparing for hearings, improved work, better communication, and the ability of the supervisor to identify how to assist an employee in doing better.

Performance standards

As a supervisor you have wrestled many times with employee evaluations. You recognize that these often represent the feelings you have about an employee's work. More often, evaluations are based on what you remember about the employee's performance—the big mistake or the great performance—or how your employee stacks up against your other employees.

Performance standards, as presented here, attempt to assist in avoiding some common rating errors. Standards are *not* employee-based. Evaluations are not based on how employees compare to one another, but rather how they are doing in relation to what is needed to get a job done. Standards allow you to separate various levels of performance by individuals, but your evaluation is based on job requirements, not individual abilities. Standards will assist you in evaluating an employee relative to the job, not to the individual's idiosyncrasies. The values and biases of the supervisor are neutralized with well-developed standards. Performance standards are not management by objectives. The goals and objectives of each individual will have a bearing on standards, but performance standards, as presented here, are well-planned and defined measures of productivity necessary to get a job done. Performance standards are a written list of job functions and related expectations that clearly define evaluation points relative to those expectations. They are developed for groups of positions performing essentially the same duties; and they must meet certain tests to be usable.

The following is a list of seven key tests good performance standards must meet:

1. Standards must be *realistic.* This simply means that the developed standards should be attainable and consistent with what is necessary to get the job done. Standards cannot work by setting the expectations so high they are impossible to reach.
2. Standards must be *specific.* They should tell the employee exactly what the expectations are and how he or she will be evaluated accordingly.
3. Standards must be *measurable.* This can be both quantitative and qualitative.

4. Standards must be *consistent with agency goals.*
5. Standards must be *challenging.* Recognition of the worker who exceeds the norm is consistent with good standards; and standards that are too easily achieved do nothing in terms of rewarding better-than-average performance.
6. Standards must be *dynamic.* As goals and objectives, technologies, operations, or experience change, so should standards.
7. Standards must be *understandable.* The employees who are going to be evaluated by your standards must understand them. Use the language of the job, for instance, if forms have numbers and all employees know them—use the numbers.

Data collection

Start the performance standard process by collecting some information about what the unit does. What kind of information on your unit's activities do you keep? Daily, weekly, or monthly tallies will assist you in identifying how much you do. If records are not maintained on some of your activities, take a sampling. For instance, if your unit answers phones, select a representative two-week period and keep track of the number of calls received. Be sure that the sample period is representative and not a peak or low time of the year. Gather all of this information and keep it ready to use.

Employee participation

Throughout this process you will be consulting with your employees—the worker experts. Their involvement will help them identify with the standards and help you ensure that the standards meet the seven guides discussed earlier.

After data collection, call a meeting of all your employees doing essentially the same work. (The number of meetings you have will depend on how varied the jobs are you supervise.) At this meeting, explain to the employees that you are developing performance standards and that you want their input. Ask them to write down everything they do. Give them a two-week deadline and explain that you will also be making a list of their tasks. Some supervisors have also requested that the employees write down what they feel are the goals and objectives of the unit or agency. When you meet with your employees at the end of the two weeks, you will undoubtedly be surprised at the results. Almost every supervisor discovers one or more of the following: (a) the list of tasks performed includes duties not being performed; (b) employees are doing things the supervisor didn't know they were doing; or (c) employees are doing things they should not be doing. If you also requested goals and objectives of the unit or agency, the answers you receive may show a real misunderstanding of what you are trying to accomplish. Some of these things

Figure 1. Developing tasks for the performance standards form.

Priority	Task	Criteria	KSA
	1. Type reports 2. Answer phones		

can be corrected right away, others may require research and time to rectify. You have not developed standards yet but the system is already reaping benefits. Take the lists given to you and condense, add, modify, and develop a list of duties for the job. Most often the list should not exceed 30 tasks and many times the list will be condensed as you go through the process.

The format

A four column form will be used to develop your standards. Column 1 is headed "Priority"; column 2—"Task"; column 3—"Criteria"; and column 4—"KSA" (knowledges, skills and abilities). The first column to be completed is #2—Task.

Take all the task statements you have collected and condensed; and place them under column #2. Figure 1 shows a partial list of tasks for a clerical job. Notice that each task is numbered and that space has been left between them.

After writing all tasks in the appropriate column, add quality statements where appropriate. There are usually some expectations regarding how well a particular task is to be performed. In the example, typing reports includes responsibility for accuracy, timeliness, and using the proper format. These appear under the task in Figure 2.

The final thing to be added to your list in the task column are *job-related* work behaviors. As an example, it may be important to have your workers be punctual, or there may be a need for use of safety equipment. Whatever the work behaviors, remember that they must be job-related and not representative of your own values. If you are the type of person who always reports to work well

Figure 2. Adding quality statements to the form.

Priority	Task	Criteria	KSA

	1. Type reports
	  a. accurately
	  b. timely
	  c. proper format
	
	2. Answer phones
	  a. timely
	  b. well		

Figure 3. Adding job-related work behaviors.

Priority	Task	Criteria	KSA

	1. Type reports
	  a. accurately
	  b. timely
	  c. proper format		

	2. Answer phones
	  a. timely
	  b. well		

	10. Punctuality		
	11. Appearance		

dressed, be sure that if this appears on your list it is a job requirement, not your personal requirement. Figure 3 adds some examples of work requirements to the list.

Now, take your list back to the employees and discuss column #2 that includes tasks, quality statements, and work behaviors. Employees' comments will help you to decide if the list is complete and if you are able to defend your work behaviors as job-related. Remember, the final decision as to whether a statement is added, eliminated, or retained is yours.

We now turn our attention to column #1, labeled "Priority." In this column we will identify the most important, less important, and incidental tasks, quality statements, and work behaviors. Mark (I) items that are of primary importance to the job. Mark (II) items that are important but less so than the primary ones; and mark (III) items that are incidental to the job. Remember to prioritize each task, each quality statement, and each work behavior. To assist you in assigning priorities, write on a separate sheet of paper a one-sentence (two at the maximum) goal, objective, reason, or capsule description of the job. Why does the job exist? What is the purpose of the job? This will assist you in prioritizing your list and discerning the important elements.

Two factors are important as you go through this exercise. First, be sure to assign a priority to *each* task, quality statement, and work behavior. Do not rank only subheadings or broad task headings. In your outline all numbers and letters receive a rank. Second, your ranking should be honest and discernible. Be sure that everything is not ranked I, because as you view the job everything is important. Refer back to your one-sentence statement as to why the job exists and relate each item to it. The priorities you establish will help you identify an employee who may be lacking in some areas but whose overall performance in the essentials of the job is satisfactory. The completion of this column rests with the supervisor and

Figure 4. Assigning priorities to each task.

Priority	Task	Criteria	KSA
I	1. Type reports		
I	a. accurately		
I	b. timely		
II	c. proper format		
II	2. Answer phones		
II	a. timely		
I	b. well		
I	10. Punctuality		
III	11. Appearance		

does not have to be taken to the employees at this time. Figure 4 shows how our example is prioritized.

Our attention now turns to column 3 "Criteria." Admittedly, this is the most difficult column to complete, for it is here that we will tell the employee what the standards are. The difficulty in filling out this column can be diminished if you remember three things: First, you have been evaluating employees all along. You are merely writing down the standards as opposed to carrying them in your head. Second, you know what has to be done. As you developed your task statements, you may have increased your knowledge of the job. Relate your standards to that knowledge. Finally, and probably most important, remember to answer two questions about each task, quality statement, and work behavior: what are the performance expectations, and how will the employee be evaluated according to those expectations?

With these things in mind, look at all the task statements that deal with quantity of work. Using the information you have previously collected on how much you do, write a figure. In our example, you know that at least 30 reports are typed a week—an average of six per day. If your data collection is done daily, your standard can be expressed daily; if weekly, then weekly, and so on. Since most jobs have slow and peak periods, use a range instead of a specific number. In our example of six reports per day, a range of four to six or three to seven may be appropriate. But whatever the range, be sure that within that range is a figure that will meet the unit's average production requirements. If more than one position is involved, the numbers in your range should be reduced. If two employees are involved, the range may be two to four reports per day. Temper this with two thoughts—what is reasonable? and can I expect the new employee to perform at this level? The answer to the latter question is usually no; so develop separate standards for the employee with less experience. The determination of when an employee's experi-

Figure 5. Developing performance criteria for tasks.

Priority	Task	Criteria	KSA
I	1. Type reports	1. 4-7 per day except employees with less than 1 year of experience, 3-5 per day.	
I	a. accurately		
I	b. timely		
II	c. proper format		
II	2. Answer phones	2. 30-35 per day	
II	a. timely		
I	b. well		
I	10. Punctuality		
III	11. Appearance		

ence equates to full performance is yours. Figure 5 adds performance standards for the quantity tasks, and includes separate standards for employees with less than one year of experience.

In developing standards for the quality statements, stand back from your list and ask yourself three helpful questions: (1) How often is the "normal" employee in this job making errors? (2) How often is it possible to "space out" a detail? (3) How critical is it to the job? Your answer to any one of these questions or all three combined can be your guide as to the acceptable error factor. Whatever the answer, remember to be realistic, use a range if applicable, and ensure that the standard is job-related.

The answers to the questions will provide you with a guide in forming a quality standard. In stating that standard, remember to tell the employee what the standard is *and* how they will be evaluated according to that standard. Some statements may not fit into a statement of numbers. In these cases, spell out how the evaluation will be made. For instance, if the general appearance of a work area is to be evaluated, set up a review of the area with the employee on a scheduled basis. By these periodic reviews of the work area, an evaluation of this category can be done based upon a review of notes taken or checklists completed. Figure 6 lists performance standards for our quality statements.

The final standards to be established are the ones related to work behaviors. In our example, punctuality is listed. You must tell the employee what the expectation is (e.g., report to work by 8:00 a.m.); and how they will be evaluated according to the standard (e.g., two late arrivals per month is acceptable). As long as the two questions are answered and your standard is job-related, the expectations will have meaning.

Figure 6. Refining the performance criteria.

Priority	Task	Criteria	KSA
I	1. Type reports	1. 4-7 per day except employees with less than 1 year of experience, 3-5 per day.	
I	a. accurately	a. 1-2 errors on finished product/more errors allowed once a week.	
I	b. timely	b. report finished one working day after receipt/2 late per week—standard	
II	c. proper format	c. typed in format given in typing manual/no improper formats accepted.	
II	2. Answers phones a. timely	2. 30-35 per day a. 1-4 rings and then answered/2×more than 4 per day—standard	
I	b. well	b. No more than 1 complaint per week from public or co-workers	
I	10. Punctuality		
III	11. Appearance		

Once you complete your standards, distribute them to your employees. During the discussions, they may be able to change your mind on specific standards. Remember, it's your responsibility to establish job-related standards and your employees are providing the test ground for them. If your standards are realistic, specific, consistent with your unit's goals, understandable, measurable, and job-related, they will stand the test. If not, make the necessary changes.

The last column, identified as KSA, is used to list the knowledges, skills, and abilities necessary to perform each task, quality statement, and work behavior. In completing this column, you take a big step in helping the employee become a better worker. As you use your standards and find an employee failing to meet them in number 1, 1c, 13, and 26b on your list, a quick glance at the KSA column for those tasks may indicate that the common characteristic in each is knowledge of agency policies and procedures. Based upon this, you can provide training to the employee in that area. Hopefully, this column will be used more than any other as you endeavor to improve production by assisting the employee in specific areas that need improvement. Figure 7 gives some examples of appropriate KSAs.

With the standards developed, you are ready to tell the employees how each category is to be reflected in the employee's overall evaluation. For instance, satisfactory performance in eight out of ten priority I tasks and five of eight priority II tasks and one of three priority III tasks will result in an overall evaluation of good. Obviously the combinations can be numerous; but a statement about how overall evaluation is arrived at is necessary. Apply your standards to whatever form your organization uses by identifying your standards and the relevant and related subfactors on your form.

The incident file

With your standards complete, you must now take one more step before implementing them. In order to keep track of your employees' performance, start an incident file. This manila folder, envelope, or notebook will be filled with notes of when the employee exceeds or fails to meet your standards. This record will assist you in evaluating your employees when the semi-annual or annual employee performance report is due. It will provide you with a complete picture of the employee's performance during the past year. Employees must know that this record is kept and it should contain any written compliments you have received about the employees. Even if there appears to be a good reason for failing to meet the standard, your incident file should include it with the reason as part of the note.

In practice, the note should contain the employee's name, the standard the employee did not meet, the date, and any explanation or reason. As you go through your file, you may observe patterns that cannot be seen as each incident develops. For instance, an employee may not be meeting one particular standard consistently because of a short staff situation. This factor, which must be taken into account in the employee's evaluation, may also affect the appraisal of other employees, your personnel budget request for next year, or how you structure your work flow. Individual patterns may be observed such as an employee who is consistently reporting late and your incident file indicates that the reason given has been a flat tire. That totals up to 15 flat tires this year. What's the real problem? Remember that this evaluation does not substitute for discipline. If there is a consistent problem, pull it out and deal with it by progressive discipline.

Figure 7. Developing KSAs for the tasks.

Priority	Task	Criteria	KSA
I	1. Type reports	1. 4-7 per day except employees with less than 1 year of experience, 3-5 per day.	1. Ability to type 40 wpm
I	a. accurately	a. 1-2 errors on finished product/ more errors allowed once a week.	a. Ability to type 40 wpm with 2 errors. Ability to proof read
I	b. timely	b. report finished one working day after receipt/2 late per week—standard	b. Ability to organize work
II	c. proper format	c. typed in format given in typing manual/no improper formats accepted.	c. Knowledge of typing manual. Ability to follow written instructions
II	2. Answers phones	2. 30-35 per day	2. Knowledge of phone usage
II	a. timely	a. 1-4 rings and then answered/2× more than 4 per day—standard	a. Knowledge of phone usage
I	b. well	b. No more than 1 complaint per week from public or co-workers	b. Ability to maintain and establish effective working relations
I	10. Punctuality	10. Report to work by 8:00 a.m./2 late per month acceptable	10. _____
III	11. Appearance	11. Dressed in clean clothes and no jeans, etc./1 complaint per month from co-workers, public or management is acceptable.	11. Knowledge of acceptable work dress

Implementation

When you have developed the standards for each group of jobs you supervise, bring all your employees together. Pass out a set of standards to each employee and explain that effective this date, everyone will be evaluated according to these standards. Also, make performance standards a portion of your new employee training.

Expect an adjustment period. Employees develop a concern of "What is management up to?" or "How will they get me with these?" They quickly realize, through experience, that the standards represent open communication from management. The job expectations are now written down, distributed, and understood. Your employees will also realize that the evaluations stemming from these standards will be consistent for everyone. No surprise evaluations occur when they thought they were doing a good job and the evaluation says otherwise. They already know how they are performing and how they will be evaluated. Finally, the outstanding employee will be evaluated as such and recognize this level of performance as having distinct characteristics from other ratings.

Your standards and all the work developing them will be well worth it. Your human relations skills will show; you've shown an interest in your employees; they've had input in the system; consistency is ensured; and you've put yourself in a good light with management. Now evaluations are not the difficult job you once thought.

Establishing Performance Goals and Standards

Development Dimensions International

Employees are usually more productive when they are committed to achieving clear and significant performance targets. Supervisors find it easier to plan work, solve problems, praise accomplishments, and evaluate performance results with measurable goals and standards. Supervisors need to know what subordinates are supposed to do, whether they did it, and how they can do it even better. And employees want to know what's expected of them, how well they are performing, and what they can do to improve their performance. Results-oriented goals and standards enable supervisors and subordinates to work more effectively and efficiently to improve performance.

Clear and measurable performance targets can save time, money, and energy because they help supervisors and employees focus on priority results. However, employees must participate in the process of developing performance goals and standards if they are to be committed to achieving defined performance targets. This article recommends a step-by-step process for establishing performance goals and targets to achieve employee cooperation and commitment.

Many organizations have attempted to develop comprehensive performance measurement systems. In some cases, those systems have been too complex to achieve the desired results. A process that

This article is adapted from a comprehensive supervisory training program called *Interaction Management* designed and published by Development Dimensions International, Pittsburgh, Pennsylvania. The program is based on a behavior modeling learning theory which relies on practice and feedback to strengthen supervisory performance. This article provides a brief overview of the concepts that are included in one module of the program which focuses on establishing performance goals/standards.

focuses on *significant* performance areas, *simple* approaches to measurement, and *specific* definition of expectations is more likely to be successful.

What are goals and standards?

Most managers, supervisors, and employees have a *feel* for what constitutes acceptable and unacceptable performance. However, because those ideas are often not communicated clearly and rarely written down, it is difficult to measure performance objectively. In many cases, the manager's "feeling" about what constitutes acceptable and unacceptable performance may not be exactly the same as the employee's "feeling." Clear definition of expectations increases the likelihood of effective performance.

What is a "goal"?   A goal is a *mutually agreed-upon,* measurable level of output. Effective goals are established through discussion and *negotiation* between a manager/supervisor and the employee.

What is a "standard"?   A standard is a *communicated,* measurable level of output. Standards are nonnegotiable. A manager or supervisor is responsible for *telling* an employee what the standards are for a particular job.

Both goals and standards are *performance outputs.* The difference lies in how they were developed. If the manager or supervisor defines the performance expectation for a particular job and tells the employee, it is a *standard.* If the manager/supervisor and employee discuss the performance expectation and negotiate the target level, it is a goal.

When do you set standards? When do you set goals?   Standards are most often communicated when there is no alternative or room for negotiation. Performance criteria may be dictated by customers, clients, regulations, political constraints, or other external influences. In other cases, employees may lack the necessary background to set goals and need to have standards set for them. It is preferable to negotiate goals with employees whenever possible. Employees are more likely to commit to achievement, share ownership, and feel that performance expectations are fair if they participate in establishing those expectations.

When is a "goal" set above or below a "standard"?   An experienced employee may set a goal to "process 33 claims a day during 1988" when the expectation is 24 claims a day. In this case, a goal was set above the standard. However, a supervisor may negotiate a goal of "19 claims a day during June" for a new and inexperienced employee. The goal was set temporarily *below* the standard until the employee gained sufficient skill to meet the unit standard.

What are some possible barriers to setting goals and standards?   So far, we have focused on the payoffs of goals and standards. There are obviously some barriers or points of resistance in any organization. Here are some typical points of resistance to setting goals/standards from three different perspectives.

Organization
We tried it before and it didn't work.
We have done okay without goals/standards.
We need to streamline things, not add more paperwork.
We just don't have enough time.
Goals/standards won't work without our present performance
   appraisal forms.

Supervisors
There are too many situations out of my control.
Our work is too difficult to measure.
Standards are too restrictive.
Priorities and assignments change.
I need to relate team goals to individual goals and that will be too
   complicated.

Employees
Might cause more problems than the process solves.
Too much record-keeping.
Can't be applied to my job.
What will I get when I meet my goals and targets?
It will expose everyone's shortcomings.
Too much pressure without rewards.

There are probably many more barriers that come to mind. While these barriers may make it difficult to introduce a meaningful process for establishing goals and standards, they don't make it impossible. The key to successful implementation is developing the skill to write meaningful goals and standards and working closely with employees to gain cooperation and commitment on the front end.

Steps for establishing performance goals and standards
There are *six* important steps for establishing performance goals/standards. They are:

1. Collect information
2. Define primary function(s)
3. Identify key result areas
4. Define areas of measurement
5. Write tentative goals and standards
6. Determine measurement and review methods.

The following sections provide a brief description of each step.

Step 1: Collect information   What data would be helpful to review when preparing to establish goals/standards? This step is important because it enables supervisors to draw from past, present, and future performance data to begin writing goals/standards. By collecting the right information at this stage, a supervisor will be able to explain to employees why the goals or standards are fair, achievable, and important. Good goals and standards are based on good information. Possible sources of information include job descriptions, past performance reviews, organizational goals and objectives, anticipated changes, employee interests, employee strengths, and organizational guidelines or regulations.

Step 2: Define primary function(s)   Why does this job exist? A function statement is a broad outline of the purpose or role of a position. It describes what services the job provides and what it does not (by omission). Function statements focus on broad targets for setting goals and standards, but do not contain goals/standards. A function statement generally remains the same from year to year, while goals/standards may change each year to respond to new priorities. There are five criteria questions to use when writing a function statement. They are:

1. What products or services are provided by this position?
2. Who receives these products or services?
3. What is unique about this position?
4. Why are these products or services provided?
5. What would be missing if this job did not exist?

A primary function statement will provide the scope, boundaries, and parameters for goal setting along with clarification of the accountabilities and uniqueness of a unit.

Step 3: Identify key result areas   What outputs or results does this unit/position provide? This step focuses on significant results as opposed to a long list of activities or responsibilities. By identifying key results, supervisors will be able to measure only the significant *few* outputs that determine success for a unit or position. Key results can be defined by first listing activities or responsibilities and then asking these criteria questions:

1.   What does the internal or external client receive?
2.   What products or services are provided?
3.   Why are the activities performed?

Step 4: Determine areas of measurement   What aspects of the key result areas are important to measure? Areas of measurement describe what must be measured in order to determine if a job has been performed successfully. Four basic areas of measurement can be applied to key result areas: *quality* (how well), *quantity* (how much), *cost* (at what expense), and *timeliness* (by when). Organization-specific areas of measurement can be established by asking questions that help define quality, quantity, cost, and timeliness.

Step 5: Write tentative goals/standards   How will you know if a goal/standard is achieved? Effective goals/standards are *measurable, understandable, achievable, controllable,* and *related to a specific time frame.*

Measurable   All outputs are probably measurable, but it is impractical to apply all areas of measurement to several key result areas. Measurements may be stated as rates (20 units per hour), ranges (70-90 units per week), or quantities per time period (90 units by September 1).

Understandable   Goals/standards must be written in terms that are clear and concise. They should use words that communicate exactly what is expected and can be understood by everyone involved.

Achievable   Unrealistic goals/standards will lead to frustration and discouragement. They may also become meaningless phrases to be ignored. Supervisors should work with employees to lower tentative goals if they seem impractical or unachievable. And supervisors must remember that what might be achievable for experienced employees may be beyond the reach of new workers.

Controllable   How can anyone be expected to submit a data report by 4 P.M. each Tuesday if the information doesn't come in until Wednesday? How can a repair technician fix a particular appliance if the parts are not available? Employees have every right to cry "unfair" if goals/standards were set in areas over which they had no control.

Related to specific time frames   Employees are motivated to reach targets that have specific deadlines. "Complete 200 units per hour" is better than "complete 200 units." If specific time periods are variable, the goal/standard can be written to reflect that variation such as "complete all studies according to agreed-upon schedules."

After establishing tentative goals/standards, supervisors may choose to rank them in order of importance. Goals/standards can be ranked by distributing 100 points among them or by using an A, B, C priority rating. Some supervisors have found it helpful to rank goals/standards from 1 to 5, with 1 being the most important. If goals/standards are to be used as a basis for evaluating performance during an annual performance appraisal, it is only fair to let an employee know in advance what is most and least important.

Step 6: Determine measurement and review methods How will you know when a goal/standard is achieved? This step is designed to help supervisors determine how to measure progress toward the goals/standards and decide when subordinates will receive feedback. By using methods of measurement that already exist, supervisors can avoid additional expenses and more paperwork. Some possible measurement methods include financial statements, productivity reports, safety reports, quality control reports, computer printouts, time cards, self logs, customer surveys, complaint logs, and observation.

When an employee will receive feedback depends on various factors including the availability of data, the type of unit or position, employee needs, and the importance of performance output. Feedback should be closely tied to the need for correcting problems or reinforcing desirable performance. Normally, feedback that is received soon after the performance is measured has the greatest impact. It is essential that the feedback process and frequency be defined when performance goals/standards are established.

PART 5

Communicating Performance Results

Performance Appraisal Interviewing for Tangible Results

——————— Barbara K. Malinauskas and Ronald W. Clement

Performance appraisal interviewing should—and can—be conducted not as a once-a-year anxiety-producing face-off but as an ongoing communication tool which balances the employee's need for supportive feedback with the organization's need to develop productive employees.

Considerable research has been done to improve performance appraisal rating formats, and much training has been conducted to reduce the errors that commonly occur in performance appraisal. However, there is less literature dealing specifically with appraisal interviewing and training for skills essential to its effectiveness. The research that is available indicates that training in the needed interview skills can facilitate the actual face-to-face communication of quality information to the employee.

Our appraisal interviewing approach—displayed in Figure 1—shows that effective performance review calls for the manager and employee to meet in three face-to-face sessions or phases called the *preview*, the *interview*, and the *review*. With continued support from the manager and expected effort by the employee, these three phases occur in an ongoing *overview* which represents the entire organization's commitment to performance appraisal.

The preview

The preview phase allows the manager to reiterate the organization's philosophy of performance appraisal; reach a mutual understanding of performance criteria; give the employee a chance to pre-

Figure 1. Performance appraisal interviewing.

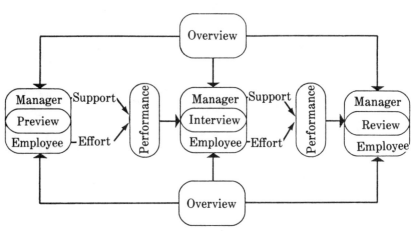

pare a self-assessment; and set the time, place, and agenda for the appraisal interview itself.

The first responsibility of the manager in the preview phase is to share the organization's philosophy of performance appraisal. The employee needs to know that providing accurate feedback, producing changes in behavior, and increasing understanding do indeed make a difference to the organization. A perception that the organization and the manager are committed to performance appraisal may increase the employee's commitment not only to this process but to improved productivity as well.

Second, the manager's performance expectations must be communicated to the employee. Ideally, such an exchange occurs soon after the employee joins the organization. The preview phase simply offers another opportunity for this information to be confirmed or updated. This significant groundwork serves to decrease later misunderstandings and provides the basis for a fair evaluation. The more clearly defined the expectations, the more likely those expectations are to be met.

Another aspect of the preview phase is providing the subordinate with a chance to engage in self-assessment. Experience with self-appraisal suggests that this practice is likely to yield a more realistic rating and a greater acceptance of the final rating by both subordinates and superiors. Specifically, employees who engage in self-assessment before an interview usually rate themselves lower, perhaps because they know an unrealistic or self-serving rating could affect their manager's perception of them. Further, some managers have found that asking subordinates to perform an initial self-appraisal encourages an open and nondefensive discussion of performance.

The third function of the preview phase is to initiate the appraisal interview itself. The manager needs to select a mutually agreeable time and adhere to it. To postpone the discussion can communicate nonverbally any number of negative messages, such as "this really isn't important."

The environment should be considered. If the discussion takes place in the manager's office—the boss' territory—the employee may feel threatened. A neutral place provides a more relaxed atmosphere with less threat of power plays. A pleasant, well-lighted meeting room might be appropriate. Ensuring the absence of interruption is also conducive to a more meaningful and focused discussion.

Finally the manager needs to prepare an agenda for the discussion. The agenda can be dictated by performance issues on the appraisal form itself or by goals set in previous appraisal sessions. Whatever the case, the agenda needs to be identified well in advance of the interview so that both participants can give careful thought to the items to be addressed. The manager might also identify specific objectives for what is to be accomplished in the interview session. For example, if the employee's performance needs significant improvement, the specific objective would be to help the employee understand the need to develop in this area. On the other hand, the objective might be to improve the relationship with the employee through more effective interaction. Whatever the objectives, if they are listed specifically, the manager can approach the interview with a sense of direction.

There also should be agreement on the order of the topics to be discussed. For example, both might agree that employee accomplishments should be addressed first to establish a positive climate for any shortcomings to be discussed later. Or the employee's view of his or her performance might precede the manager's to allow for a more equal footing in the interview.

The overriding objective of the preview phase is to set the stage for the performance discussion itself—what we have called the interview phase. Meeting this objective requires thorough preparation and planning on the part of both parties.

The interview

The interview is a face-to-face meeting between manager and employee held primarily to exchange ideas. Neither party should actually conduct the interview; both need to experience it. The interview process can be a complex, potentially emotional interaction. Latent with the possibility for perceptual differences, defensiveness, and conflict, the interview can result in faulty listening, misunderstandings, and even hostility. Those who need development the most may learn the least. The research literature shows quite clearly that training in relevant communication skills is essential to overcoming these potential problems.

An understanding of the nature of communication not only improves the probability that such training will work, but also helps to outline the necessary training areas. First of all, communication skills can be learned in training. Courses on listening, speaking, and nonverbal communication are not a new phenomenon in the world of work. Second, communication is a two-way process, the success of which is dependent upon these very skills. Third, even though two people are not engaged in a verbal exchange, communication still occurs nonverbally.

Training for effective communication in the performance appraisal interview needs to consider verbal, listening, and nonverbal skills in the ways outlined below.

Verbal skills   These are used primarily in giving feedback to the employee.

Positive versus negative   Choice of language should be an initial consideration. Terms chosen to discuss the employee's performance should not only be specific, concrete, and behavior-oriented but also should be positive in nature. Words such as "shortcoming," "failure," and "deficiency" are much more threatening than positive words such as "growth," "development," and "progress."

Supportive versus defensive   The appropriate verbal skills on the part of the supervisor can produce a supportive climate for the appraisal interview. The potential for defensiveness in both parties is great, and the building of defenses diminishes concentration and increases the chance of the message being distorted. Proper language can reduce the defensiveness of the communication situation. Research in this area shows that a climate of openness is created by using words that are, among other things, descriptive rather than evaluative, spontaneous rather than manipulative, and emphatic rather than indifferent.

For example, evaluative or judgmental speech increases defensiveness: "You never get your reports in on time." Descriptive speech, on the other hand, perceived as a genuine request for information, contributes to a supportive climate: "I've noticed that your last two reports weren't turned in on time. Is there a problem?" Communication that conveys empathy for feelings and respect for the worth of the listener is also supportive: "We all make mistakes like that. That's quite understandable. I'm glad you told me about it."

Listening skills   Whereas verbal skills deal primarily with the content of a message, listening skills often reflect the emotional dimension of the interview situation. Emotions range from the employee's eagerness to hear about a job well done to fear of being raked over the coals. The supervisor needs to listen and respond to these emotions. If the superior listens to understand how the subordinate feels about certain issues, there is less likelihood of becoming judgmental and producing a defensive climate.

Paraphrasing   One skill especially critical to listening empathically is paraphrasing, in which the listener restates what he believes the speaker has just said. For example, if the employee says, "I can't get reports in on time when nobody else is doing his job," then the manager might paraphrase: "You're saying that meeting deadlines is difficult when you have to rely on other people in your department." Paraphrasing indicates the manager has been listening, which in turn grants the employee a sense of worth. It also provides an opportunity to check the manager's perception of what's just been said. If there is a misunderstanding, it can be remedied quickly.

Effective questioning   The ability to question effectively helps a manager get necessary information or provide clarification. An awareness of two types of questions—open and closed—and their potential responses should be part of the manager's communication repertoire. Open-ended questions such as "How do you account for this?" or "What could we do to reduce those costs?" allow the employee an opportunity to share fully his or her thoughts and feelings. Closed questions such as "Did you finish that prospectus?" or "How long have you been with us, Harold?" require short answers which tend to diminish employee input into the discussion. Knowing when to use each type of question is a significant communication skill which can be developed through training.

Monitoring   The manager needs to monitor the amount of listening that's done in the performance review. The tendency is to hold court and judge, in which case listening is minimal. If, however, the manager has allowed the employee to engage in self-assessment and has encouraged the employee to come to the interview with concerns or problems, the employee has reason to believe that there will be a discussion and an opportunity to be heard.

Recent research suggests that employees are more satisfied with their appraisal interviews and with their superiors when they participate more in the appraisal process, especially in the interview itself. Training in the needed listening skills can help to assure that the supervisor can successfully involve the employee in the discussion.

Nonverbal skills   While verbal communication skills are content-oriented, and listening deals primarily with emotions, nonverbal skills supply emphasis to both.

Body language   During the performance appraisal interview, the manager should be aware, first of all, of his or her own body. Many features of the body—posture, gestures, facial expression, and eye contact—often speak louder than words. During the performance review, for example, the manager might lean slightly forward to encourage an employee's participation. Maintaining substantial eye contact without staring serves a similar function by indicating the manager is paying attention and focusing on the employee. Frequent breaking of eye contact—looking away—indicates disinterest and may inhibit the other individual.

Paralanguage   Paralanguage refers to a wide range of vocal characteristics including the inflection of words and the tone of the voice. This nonverbal feature can communicate the sincerity of the message conveyed. In other words, how something is said often determines whether or not the listener believes it to be true. For example, "I'm so pleased with the proposal you turned in last week" can be said with correct paralanguage to indicate an honest appreciation of good work. However, by a different tone of voice and inflection of words, this same statement can communicate sarcasm.

Space language   Where the manager sits during the interview—whether behind a desk or in a chair next to the employee—communicates a definite message. The desk separates the two and reminds the subordinate of status differences between them. Sitting side-by-side with the chairs turned slightly to allow easy eye contact will communicate a more equal footing and might encourage increased participation from the employee.

In addition to using appropriate nonverbal cues, the supervisor also needs to interpret the employee's nonverbal communication. Through careful observation, the manager can "read" the employee's facial expression, eye movements, and posture. These cues may indicate tension, misunderstanding, or disagreement. They may even contradict what the employee has said, calling for the manager to tactfully investigate the discrepancy. For example: "You've indicated things are going well with the departmental reorganization, and yet the look on your face and the way you said this tells me you're not really sure. Is there something else you think I should know?" Checking out the nonverbal message with the employee allows an opportunity for clarification and better understanding. Further, along with the verbal and listening skills mentioned earlier, nonverbal skills can and should be developed through training.

The manager's use of these verbal, listening, and nonverbal skills enables the two parties to accomplish the interview objectives and to complete the agenda set forth in the preview session. Through nondirective, open-ended questioning, the manager encourages the subordinate to share his or her ideas and listens empathically for the employee's concerns and feelings, watchful of nonverbal signals which indicate tension, anxiety, or disagreement.

In a free and open discussion, areas for improvement can be determined, and goals can be set for the future. These goals include those the manager sets to support the employee's efforts. It is critical that the interview lead to a concrete plan for performance development. The discussion might end with a summary of what's been discussed and a restatement of the commitments both have made for the future.

The review

The review phase allows the manager and the employee to meet on a more informal basis—perhaps as soon as a month after the appraisal interview—to reflect on the goals which had been previously set. This meeting can be initiated by either of the two people, depending on their relationship. If the employee is experienced and the relationship is based on trust and openness, the employee might want to take the responsibility for initiating the review. This assumption of responsibility increases the employee's commitment and the likelihood that performance as well as satisfaction will be improved. If the employee is inexperienced, or if the relationship has not yet developed to the point of trust and openness, the manager may want to initiate the review, with the understanding that the employee will take on that responsibility in the future.

The concept of the review phase arises from the literature that suggests providing feedback or reinforcement for improved performance should be an ongoing rather than a more threatening, infrequent, periodic activity. Perhaps more important, frequent discussion of progress allows the two parties to stay in touch with regard to the goals set in the interview phase. Are those goals still realistic? Have conditions changed?

For example, assignments may have been added to the employee's workload, or the resources originally depended upon may have become scarce. People change, too, and how the employee felt on the day of the interview may no longer reflect present feelings. What seemed like a good idea then may no longer have his or her full commitment. The review phase offers the opportunity to reflect on that change in attitude.

The overview

The performance appraisal interview can improve any organization's performance appraisal system. But like a carpenter's tool, its value alone is limited. To reach the carpenter's final objective—the construction of a building—the tools must be used in conjunction with other tools and, of course, other skilled tradespeople such as electricians and plumbers.

So it is with the performance appraisal interview. In and of itself, its value is limited. Research shows that ". . . reactions to appraisal sessions do not occur in a vacuum. They fit into the overall perception of the work experience."[1] This perception of the appraisal interview is colored by the climate of the organization. "When the climate is one of high trust, support, and openness, appraisers and subordinates alike see performance appraisal as going better."[2] Both of these instances report greater emphasis on the subordinate's development and greater participation and constructive contribution during the interview.

The organizational climate also must reflect a commitment to performance appraisal from higher organizational levels. This commitment can help determine whether supervisors are committed to performance appraisal and whether they will spend the time and effort to do it well. Higher-level managers also must become role models for the appraising behavior they wish lower level superiors to exhibit. A supervisor tends to mirror the management style and behavior of his or her boss.

Guided by the manager, the performance appraisal interview should also occur in an environment based on the concept of integration, whereby both the individual's needs and the organization's objectives are considered. Through mutual goal setting and by providing opportunity for feedback and growth, the manager helps the employee to identify more with the organization and the need for it to be successful.

To realize the full potential of the performance appraisal process—motivating and improving performance, strengthening superior-subordinate relations, and diagnosing individual and organizational problems—the interview must be approached not in a vacuum, but within the overall climate of the organization.

1. Ilgen, D.R., R.B. Peterson, B.A. Martin, and D.A. Boeschen. "Supervisor and Subordinate Reactions to Performance Appraisal Sessions." *Organizational Behavior and Human Performance* 23(3):311-330.

2. Lawler, E.E., A.M. Mohrman, and S.M. Resnick, "Performance Appraisal Revisited." *Organizational Dynamics* 13(1):31-35.

The Performance Appraisal Interview: What, When, and How?

Ronald W. Clement and George E. Stevens

Performance appraisal is an increasingly important personnel practice in both the public and private sectors. In public employment at the federal level, the major impetus for the recent emphasis on performance appraisal has been the Civil Service Reform Act of 1978. This Act calls for performance appraisal systems that will encourage employee participation in setting performance standards and that will also communicate job requirements to employees.[1] Further, the Act specifies that performance appraisals are to form the basis for training and placement decisions and will determine the pay and other benefits of GS-13 through GS-15 managers and of the Senior Executive Service.[2]

However, there also have been attempts to improve performance appraisal at other levels of government. For example, a 1975 revision of the charter of New York City mandated the installation of a new performance appraisal system for middle and senior-level managers.[3] Also, at least fourteen states have attempted to improve employee productivity by basing merit pay raises on a more systematic appraisal of performance.[4] Recent judicial decisions emphasizing the rights of individual employees indicate that concern for performance appraisal will continue to grow in the public sector.[5]

Recent court decisions also suggest a renewed interest in performance appraisal in the private sector. Federal courts have ruled that performance appraisal is subject to the same regulations as employment tests and the selection process in general.[6] Consequently, a growing number of court cases dealing with this personnel activity is likely. One aspect of performance appraisal that has become especially important in recent years is the interview during which performance is reviewed. For example, a review of recent judicial decisions involving charges of discrimination shows that a key variable is the degree of communication between employer and employee. In other words it must be demonstrated that performance appraisal results have been reviewed with the employee.[7] Similarly, the requirements of the Civil Service Reform Act for employee participation and for the communication of critical job elements to employees are clear indicators of the need for discussion between superior and employee.

Although a great deal of research has been done on the performance appraisal interview over the past ten years, no one source has pulled this information together for use by those who actually conduct performance appraisals: the managers of today's organizations. This research has led to some excellent models to guide academic studies but has not been summarized or widely distributed for the benefit of practitioners. This situation is especially unfortunate in view of the problems found in current interviewing practices. A common problem is that supervisors and their employees often cannot even agree on whether or not an interview was held.[8] What the supervisor considers a performance review may be nothing more than a brief comment in the hallway to the employee. Apparently, the "vanishing performance appraisal" still is a reality in organizational life. A second interviewing problem is that, even when both agree that the review was held, they often differ in their opinions on the level of performance credited to the employee.[9] Alternative explanations for this phenomenon are that the employee tends to hear only favorable comments, rejecting those that are less favorable, or that the supervisor avoids discussing negative evaluations because doing so is unpleasant.

Research shows quite clearly that the way in which the interview is conducted may be much more important than other aspects of the appraisal process, including the technique used as the basis for employee evaluation. For example, although behavioral techniques have been found to be more accurate than those which focus on personnel traits, both types are considerably more accurate when raters have been properly trained.[10] Training can improve the supervisor's ability to conduct the interview and might best include both employees and supervisors. Both parties need to learn how to overcome the defensive climate that can exist in this process.[11]

One can only speculate on the reasons why the abundance of scholarly research on performance appraisal interviews has not been made available as practical sources for managers. Perhaps scholars share the view that more research needs to be done; therefore, to make sweeping recommendations at this time would be premature. Generally, this line of thought is most appropriate with regard to scientific inquiry. However, management researchers have been criticized recently for failing to address practitioner concerns better and for not translating theory into application soon enough.[12] The complaint is that many researchers are too concerned about scientific rigor and tend to distance themselves from applied problems. Perhaps a better balance is needed between the scholarly desire for tested theory and the practical need to improve current managerial practice. The most useful theories are not necessarily those that have been most thoroughly tested; a recent survey of management researchers shows that the perceived importance of a theory is not related to its empirical validity.[13]

A model of the interview process

The purpose here is to describe a situational approach to the performance appraisal interview. The approach is based largely on the available research evidence and may be used as a broad guide for managers in various performance evaluation situations. The model, shown in Figure 1, focuses on three dimensions of the performance appraisal interview that need to be addressed by practitioners: (1) frequency—how often to conduct a review; (2) criteria—what performance areas to focus on; and (3) style—how to conduct the review, especially the degree of participation to allow. In addition, this situational approach identifies the types of variables the manager should consider in deciding what approach to use in an interview. These variables include the purpose of the review, characteristics of both the employee and the supervisor, and the nature of the job as well as those organizational features that relate to personnel policies.

The model proposed here does not consider variables unrelated to the appraisal interview. For example, despite the importance of the technique used and the abundance of research on performance appraisal methodology, this topic is beyond the scope of the present article and, as mentioned earlier, may not be as important as the interview style itself. Also, we do not present information on how raters may be trained to reduce common rating errors, a topic covered exclusively elsewhere.[14] Finally, the model is not proposed as a "cookbook" approach to performance reviews; the supervisor using this model still must diagnose the variables identified by the model in order to decide the best interview approach to use in a given situation.

The frequency of review

The availability evidence indicates that the typical performance review is conducted annually.[15] For example, in one extensive survey

Figure 1. A situational approach to the performance appraisal interview.

Variables influencing the review	Dimensions of the review
Purpose of the review	

Employee characteristics
    Level of experience
    Performance level
    Needs
    Etc.
	Frequency of review

Characteristics of the supervisor
    Level of experience
    Skill in appraisal
    Needs
    Etc.
	Criteria discussed
	    Performance outcomes
	    Job behaviors

Features of the job itself
    Routineness
    Clarity
    Newness
    Etc.
	Style of interview
	    Autocratic
	    Participative

Organizational variables
    Climate
    Time available for review
    Organizational policies
    Etc.	

covering office employees, managers, and production workers in 150 industrial and governmental organizations, about ninety percent of the respondents reported using formal yearly performance appraisals including a review of the results with the employee. More recent thinking indicates that performance reviews should be conducted more often than once per year, with the actual frequency dependent upon the situation.[16]

Purpose of the review The first situational variable is the purpose of the review. (See Figure 1.) Reviews conducted for the purpose of employee development probably need to be held more frequently than those aimed at determining employee rewards, such as pay increases. Trying to reach both objectives in a single interview leads to two kinds of conflict.[17] The first involves the conflict experienced by the supervisor between the roles of judge and helper. In evaluating an employee for reward determination, the supervisor is forced to make difficult judgments that affect the employee's future. Conversely, the developmental focus calls for the role of a coach or helper. Most supervisors probably resolve this conflict in favor of the judgmental role, largely because their time and their control over employee rewards are both limited. If one can give an employee only a 7 percent pay increase when the latter has really earned 10, then one is tempted to judge the employee's performance more harshly. A second and larger conflict, however, is that between individual and organizational goals in performance appraisal. On the one hand, the organization wants valid information about its employees, information that may be used to improve their performance. However, the employee wants to maintain a certain positive self-image and to obtain just rewards. As long as employees see the appraisal process as a threat to their rewards, careers, or self-image, they will be reluctant to communicate openly and provide valid information. Separating the developmental and reward evaluations would allow for more open communication at least in the former type of review.

Employee characteristics   In addition to splitting the reward component from the developmental review, it may be necessary to conduct the latter more frequently than once per year. This is especially true for employees who are less experienced or who perform poorly.[18] Such employees generally need more frequent guidance to get them "on track" if they are to meet the supervisor's standards. Furthermore, newer and less experienced employees are more likely to feel dependent upon feedback from the supervisor and to respond favorably to frequent reviews. In fact, a number of management consultants recommend that periodic coaching sessions be conducted.

Employee variables (such as the employee's personality and needs) are just as important as an employee's skill level and experience. Employees who are more confident and open probably can handle frequent developmental discussions better than those who lack self-esteem.[19] A higher level of confidence allows these employees to feel less threatened by discussions of their performance weaknesses. Further, upwardly mobile employees generally desire frequent feedback in order to be sure they are maintaining their desired "fast-track" pace. For these types of employees, uncorrected or repeated errors can reduce their mobility.

A matter of concern is what to do about the employee who feels threatened by frequent performance reviews but whose level of performance or skill calls for more evaluation sessions. The issue here should perhaps best be decided in favor of more reviews, with the success of the effort dependent upon the supervisor's skill in conducting performance reviews.

Characteristics of the supervisor The needs and skills of the supervisor should be considered in deciding how often to conduct a performance review. Research indicates that this process often can be as unpleasant for the boss as it is for the employee.[20] Giving negative feedback can be as unpleasant as receiving it; accordingly, some supervisors will tend to review an employee's performance less frequently than might be desired. Aside from the interpersonal threat, it is also evident that supervisors dislike the paperwork usually associated with performance appraisal and/or do not see how the performance evaluation task can help them in their work. (These two barriers hampered the implementation of the new performance appraisal system in New York City that was mentioned earlier.) One way to overcome these problems is to provide for participative approaches to appraisal and to train supervisors how to use them. Use of participation often can take some of the evaluation pressure off the supervisor and place it on the employees, who in fact may have a more accurate view of their performances. Often the supervisor discovers that the employee's self-rating is compatible with what the former would have proposed in the first place.

A related issue is the supervisor's skill in conducting the review. No doubt those with little skill in this regard will try to avoid this personnel activity. A process as complex as the performance appraisal interview can be frustrating for a supervisor lacking the required ability. Again, training the supervisor in how to conduct a meaningful performance review seems to be the solution here. As was suggested earlier, it might be effective to train the employees and supervisor together in order to provide a greater transfer of learning. And it is probably worth noting that behavior modeling is an especially effective approach to use in this type of training. This fairly recent addition to training methodology, described in detail elsewhere, includes modeling of the desired behavior, role playing by trainees, and methods for transferring the training to the job.[21]

Features of the job and organization Job and organizational variables to consider when deciding how often to conduct a review are relatively straightforward. Simply put, the less routine and the more ambiguous the task at hand, the more frequent should be the performance reviews to ensure that the employee is indeed "on track."[22] Especially when the supervisor is also uncertain about where the job should be headed, it is important for the two parties to communicate frequently about the different possibilities. Likewise, the newer the task or job to the employee and to the organization, the more often performance appraisals should be held. Establishing new standards and expectations requires frequent discussion.

Organizational variables include the climate within the organization, the time available for performance reviews and the policies of the organization with regard to this personnel activity. Organizational climate is a concept that received much attention in the management literature during the 1970's, but today it is largely ignored. Perhaps the reason is that the concept is hard to define and therefore to measure.[23] Nevertheless, it can be a useful concept when explained and used properly. Basically, it refers to the atmosphere within an organization, especially the relationship between labor and management, as perceived by the members: "Organizational climate is a relatively enduring quality of the internal environment of an organization that (a) is experienced by its members, (b) influences their behavior, and (c) can be described in terms of the values ... of the organization."[24] If employees on the whole tend to regard management and the organization as friendly, caring, and considerate, then the climate is good. On the other hand, if a feeling of distrust and suspicion prevails, with each side expecting the other to seek only its own ends, then the climate is poor.

When the organizational climate is poor, performance appraisal can be a very unpleasant process. The prospect of facing skeptical or even belligerent employees might tend to make a supervisor want to skip this personnel activity. However, a long lapse of time between reviews probably increases the employee's fear and distrust of the boss and the entire review process. More frequent developmental evaluations should actually improve the climate while also improving employee performance. Of course, simply increasing the frequency might not be enough. In addition, employee participation in the development of the appraisal system, plus adequate training of supervisors in the use of the new system, may further enhance the performance review process.

A common complaint of supervisors is the lack of time to conduct performance appraisals. On the one hand, more frequent reviews could improve both performance and the supervisor-employee relationship to such an extent that the interview session eventually would become shorter and there could even be a tapering off on their frequency; on the other hand, there are situations where the time for review simply does not exist, in which case reality calls for less frequent but longer interviews. The policies of top management obviously play a major role here. If higher levels of management emphasize more frequent schedules of review, provide support for training in performance appraisal, and allocate rewards on the basis of how often supervisors conduct reviews, then many of the obstacles to frequent reviews simply fall by the wayside. Again, with reference to New York, a lack of top management support was yet another variable hampering the new performance appraisal system there. More specifically, managers were not given the means to reward or punish subordinates as an outcome of performance evaluation, and agency heads would not commit key staff members to the program.

The criteria on which to focus

The one performance appraisal area about which researchers have largely agreed is the criteria to be discussed in an evaluation interview. Despite the tendency of managers to rely upon employee traits and characteristics such as initiative and maturity, the evidence shows that a focus upon job behavior and employee outcomes for the organization are far better measures of performance. Not only are traits subjective and difficult to change, but trait-based appraisals also fail to be defensible legally in court cases charging discrimination in performance reviews.[25]

Ideally, the review discussion should focus upon both behaviors and outcomes, for usually neither alone completely describes performance.[26] An employee can act out the correct behaviors, going "through the motions" so to speak, without really accomplishing anything of import on the job. Conversely, desired outcomes certainly can be obtained through improper and unethical behaviors.

There are some situations, however, where a supervisor might have to (or want to) emphasize either behavior or outcomes. Again, the variables that come into play are the purpose of the review and the characteristics of the subordinate, the supervisor, the job, and the organization. With regard to the purpose of the review, one might lean toward employee outcomes or accomplishments when deciding upon rewards. Top management is more likely to support a recommendation for a pay increase when it is backed by evidence of results on the job. However, for purposes of employee development, a focus upon specific job behaviors probably is the best approach to use.[27] To improve job behavior, one must discuss specific behaviors; telling a salesperson to "get more sales" is not nearly as helpful as telling him or her specifically how to close a sale more effectively.

Employee characteristics Employee variables important in the decision of which criteria to discuss are the dependability of the employee, the extent to which the employee controls his or her work, and the level of independence the subordinate prefers.[28] The manager might tend to focus primarily upon outcomes as opposed to behaviors when the employee can be trusted to act properly and has a great deal of control over outcomes. The dependable employee who also has a great deal of control over outcomes tends to know exactly what is required to achieve those outcomes. Examples include punch-press operators in a manufacturing plant and claims processors in an insurance company. Further, failure to achieve the desired outcomes in such cases usually means that correct behaviors were not used. In a similar vein, outcomes often can be the criteria of focus for employees who desire a great deal of independence, especially if they also have a high level of competence.

The problem is that the performance of most employees depends to a large extent upon that of others. In this more typical situation, it can be unfair to hold an employee totally responsible for unsatisfactory results; the work of other parties must also be taken into account.

Characteristics of the supervisor Certain characteristics of the supervisor also might pinpoint relevant criteria upon which to focus in the review. Two key variables here might be the amount of experience and the level of skill possessed by the supervisor in conducting performance evaluations. The more experienced and/or skilled the supervisor, the more likely he or she can lean toward an analysis of outcomes in the review. The experienced or skilled supervisor can usually judge, based upon the outcomes achieved, whether or not the correct behaviors were used by the subordinate. For example, an experienced manufacturing superintendent probably could tell from the productivity levels whether or not the employee had also properly maintained the equipment used to produce that outcome. A less skilled manager might need to observe and evaluate specific behaviors to understand better why certain performance levels were reached.

A final supervisory variable of concern here is more controversial: the need of the supervisor to control the situation. Management researchers have tended to believe that the supervisor should be able to apply the "best" management style depending upon the situation at hand, with the situation largely determined by the task, the larger organization, and the employee. Only recently has it been recognized that the supervisor also has needs to be met in this determination.[29] Generally speaking, a supervisor who needs to be very much in control will tend to focus on both behavior and outcomes in performance review. In fact, this "control" variable will likely override all the others, whether or not it should.

Features of the job The nature of the job is a key variable in determining what criteria to examine in a given performance review. For example, the results achieved by a public relations specialist often are so nebulous that the supervisor is doing well just to make sure the individual is at least using correct behaviors. At the other extreme, a sales manager simply cannot observe certain critical behaviors performed by salespeople and may have to rely upon sales results as a measure of this area of their performance. The two job variables upon which these examples focus are ability to quantify results and the opportunity to observe behavior on the job. When one cannot quantify outcomes, one must rely more upon behaviors performed; when behaviors cannot be observed, one must identify those results which generally indicate proper performance. Fortunately, in some situations where behavior cannot be observed directly, the supervisor can rely upon the observations of others—for example, the customers of some salespeople.

Two other variables of considerable importance are the clarity of the task to be performed and the newness of the job to the organization. The manager probably should lean toward outcomes as opposed to behaviors for jobs that are non-routine.[30] Simply put, the less routine the job, the less likely one is able to identify the specific behaviors to be performed; one simply must leave it to the employee to decide what actions are appropriate in achieving the desired results. On the other hand, the newer the job is to the organization, the more likely management will want to specify the exact steps to be followed until employees eventually fall into a predictable routine. A final job variable to consider is the extent to which it is possible to identify individual outcomes.[31] Some jobs involve a group effort in which it is not feasible to single out the achievements of any one member of the group. In this case, the supervisor may have to deal with specific job behaviors or allocate rewards based on group performance.

Organizational variables The final set of variables affecting the criteria on which to focus in performance appraisal lies within the larger organization itself. Once again, the key variables are: the time available for performance appraisal, the climate within the organization, and the policies of top management with regard to performance review. The influences of the "time" variable is fairly obvious and practical: a supervisor who has little time available for the appraisal process will probably emphasize outcomes over behaviors. Although the supervisor may want to observe and evaluate job behaviors, the time to do so, as dictated by the number of subordinates to be reviewed or the nature of the manager's job itself, may not be available. The time required for appraisals largely determines whether or not supervisors will actually try to help the process work. A new performance appraisal system imposed upon supervisors at a county Metropolitan Transit Authority failed to achieve acceptance by those supervisors largely because of the time element.[32] The new system required each supervisor to write a lengthy narrative each quarter on each of 30 subordinates, whereas the old system, jointly approved by supervisors, employees, and the union, merely involved the completion of a checklist. To cope with the new system, supervisors developed a standard narrative for an "outstanding" employee and submitted it for all employees.

One caution is in order here, however. Some supervisors feel they never have enough time to conduct thorough performance reviews with their subordinates, largely due to the complex nature of their own jobs. They argue that their jobs involve more than the simple functional approach described in many management textbooks. However, the investment of time in frequent and full performance appraisals often can mean fewer performance problems to worry about later. The end result should be a savings in time for the manager.

Organizational climate is another variable of concern, and quite simply, the worse the climate the more likely it is that *both* behaviors and outcomes should be measured in performance appraisals.[33] With a poor climate, an emphasis only upon outcomes could lead to the exclusion of means; unethical and improper behaviors would likely result. Likewise, a focus largely upon behavior might tend to lead employees to simply "go through the motions." But a focus upon both behaviors and outcomes might actually improve the climate over the long run. A fuller knowledge of the problems faced by subordinates could lead to a better understanding between the two parties.

Finally, the policies of top management have a rather obvious influence upon the appraisal process at every level of the organization. Specifically, if top management rewards supervisors for conducting thorough reviews, including concern for employees' developmental needs, then supervisors are more likely to observe and evaluate both behaviors and outcomes. Conversely, if top management places strict emphasis upon the results expected of lower level managers, such as quarterly sales or monthly production, then managers will focus upon outcomes as opposed to the behaviors required to achieve those outcomes. This "output" approach to management control, so typical of U.S. companies, has been cited as one of the major reasons why foreign competition has done so well in markets that used to be American-dominated.[34] In short, too much emphasis on short-term results has in many cased led to a sacrifice of long-term development.

The interview style

In performance evaluation, the style of the interview can range all the way from totally non-participative (autocratic) to very participative. In the latter the employee largely controls the process. Although management researchers have been accused of favoring participation to the total exclusion of autocratic methods, in reality the evidence from such research shows that autocratic management styles do have their place.[35] At the same time, recent research shows that both employees and their supervisors tend to favor participative approaches to performance review.[36] The degree of participation to allow in a given situation is again a function of the purpose of the review as well as the characteristics of the employee, the supervisor, the job, and the organization.

As we explained earlier, the two broad purposes of performance appraisal are to determine the rewards due employees and to decide upon their developmental needs. Generally speaking, the latter calls for a participative approach to the review. The supervisor alone is unlikely to have a complete understanding of the employee's job or performance, and the best alternative source of information is the employee. Further, employees are more likely to accept the results of the discussion regarding developmental needs if they participate. Participation is well-tested and widely-accepted approach to overcoming resistance to change.[37]

In the determination of rewards due the employee, the decision regarding the use of participation is not so clear-cut. There is some evidence that the higher the degree of threat in the context of the interview, the better the employee will respond to an autocratic style.[38] Certainly the "reward" appraisal tends to be more threatening than an evaluation for developmental purposes. Aside from the threat factor, there also is the situation in which the reward (e.g., pay increase, promotion) has been decided in advance by higher management. Here, a non-participative approach again is probably best because participation might lead the employee falsely to believe that the decision still can be influenced. On the other hand, organizations with a more open climate would probably find it useful to start this reward process at the bottom and first obtain the employee's input. Management still can retain the right to make the final decision, but with intelligent input from employees on their evaluations as to self-worth.

Employee characteristics As in the case of the frequency of review, the level of participation varies with the amount of experience the employee has and the extent to which he or she is dependent upon the supervisor for performance feedback.[39] Clearly, newer and less experienced employees tend to rely more heavily upon the boss for feedback on performance quality and might even feel threatened by a request to evaluate their own performance. On the other hand, experienced employees might be offended by a an autocratic approach and often have opinions and observations regarding their performance that their boss could not possibly have. Recent research shows that the supervisor and the employee each tend to observe different yet valid features of the latter's performance.[40] Certainly for developmental evaluations the supervisor would be wise to provide for substantial self-evaluation by subordinates who probably are most knowledgeable about their own performance behaviors.[41]

Characteristics of the supervisor Supervisory variables to consider in determining the degree of participation include the amount and kinds of power the supervisor has over the employee, the extent to which the supervisor feels threatened by the performance appraisal process, the supervisor's skill in handling employee participation, and the supervisor's level of experience. The more relative power the supervisor has, the more likely an autocratic approach will work. However, an analysis of the supervisor's power must consider the several bases of that power: the ability to control rewards and punishments, knowledge of the employee's work, the personality of the supervisor, and his or her connections to those in power.[42] For example, a supervisor lacking the power to hire and fire, or a supervisor who really does not understand the work of an important subordinate probably needs to allow the employee more input into the performance evaluation process.

The threat of the performance evaluation process to the supervisor is a recently recognized phenomenon in management research. For many years, it was assumed that employees were the only ones threatened due to the impact of evaluations on their salaries and careers. Supervisors also are threatened, but for different reasons. First of all, the necessity of giving negative feedback is seldom a pleasant process. In fact, one of the reasons for the lack of agreement between supervisors and employees on what was said during a review is the former's reluctance to discuss negative feedback: employees leave the review feeling that they have done better than they really have.[43] Secondly, the evaluation of performance requires the exercise of power by the supervisor, regardless of the nature of the feedback, and many simply are not comfortable with this role. The result is that many supervisors lean toward an autocratic approach in order to get the process over as quickly as possible. As was suggested earlier, a better approach might be to provide the supervisor with training in how to conduct a participative review. The training itself might alleviate the reluctance to give negative feedback, and the use of greater participation would tend to equalize the power balance during the review.

Another supervisory variable influencing the degree of participation is the supervisor's skill in using this approach to performance review. Although there might be a tendency to assume that any supervisor can learn to use participative methods, this assumption simply is false. First, interpersonal job behavior can be hard to change, as was discovered in the earlier uses of sensitivity training.[44] Further testimony to the difficulty of changing interpersonal job behavior is the leader "match" concept, which suggests placing leaders in situations compatible with their different styles instead of trying to change the style itself.[45] Second, even if the supervisor could learn to use participative methods with appropriate training, such training may not be available. Despite the growth of the training field over the last twenty years, there undoubtedly still is a shortage of the needed courses in many organizations.

Finally, the supervisor's level of experience in managing others is an important variable to consider in the participation decision. Specifically, research shows that less experienced supervisors tend to blame the employee for poor performance even when environmental variables beyond the employee's control are the real culprits.[46] The lesson here is that newer supervisors might gain a more accurate reading of employee performance by involving the latter in the evaluation.

Features of the job   Job variables affecting the use of participation include the clarity of the task, the newness of the job, and the level of professionalism involved. Simply put, the less clear the task or the newer the job is to the organization, the more likely that participative methods of review are needed. It is just these types of situations where two-way discussion is needed to clear up differences of opinion and for both parties to learn what the job really involves. A good example is the implementation of a new computerized record and reporting system. Even if the organization has had experience with computers, the managers of those working directly with the new system cannot possibly know how the jobs in question will change. Too many unexpected problems occur in the first few months. Regarding the level of professionalism, the research evidence shows quite clearly that employees who are knowledgeable and independent—two features characteristic of professional personnel—respond well to a participative style of appraisal.[47] A key reason why teachers and nurses have turned to unionism over the past two decades has been a lack of participation in formulating the personnel policies that affect them.

Organizational variables   Several organizational variables affect the decision as to what style to use in evaluation interviews. Included are the time available for the review, management policies regarding performance evaluation, the climate within the organization, and the legal pressures being faced by the organization. The influence of time upon the use of participation has long been recognized in organizational research, and the conclusion here is quite practical and simple: use participation only when the time for it is available.[48] The more pressured the supervisor and employee are and the larger the number of employees the supervisor has to evaluate, the less likely participative approaches will be used. Upper management can influence this decision, and certainly the more management pushes for participative approaches, provides training in those approaches, and rewards supervisors for using them, the more likely the latter will find the time for the reviews.

To a large extent, the question of whether the supervisor will set aside the necessary time and whether top management will emphasize the use of participation will be determined by the climate within the organization. Generally speaking, the better the climate between management and employees, the more likely participative methods of review will be used. Supervisors and employees are more likely to discuss matters on an equal footing when they get along well. However, as we mentioned earlier, participative performance appraisal can be one of the means to improve the climate within the organization, especially when supervisors and managers are properly trained in such techniques.

The final organizational variable is the legal situation facing the organization. Earlier it was stated that a major reason for the growth in the importance and use of performance review was the legal pressure to improve this process in public as well as private employment. For example, a central feature of the Civil Service Reform Act of 1978 was the use of participation in performance evaluation. And a review of recent court cases on discrimination in performance evaluation shows that the defendant company is more likely to prevail when its performance appraisal system allows for input from the employee. In general, there is growing pressure for participative performance review in most organizations, and those organizations which recognize the need to develop legally defensible performance appraisal procedures would be wise to audit their review systems.

Conclusion

The emphasis on performance appraisal in both the public and private sectors is likely to continue in the near future. The evidence for this includes recent court decisions and actions at all three levels of government, especially the passage of the Civil Service Reform Act of 1978.

Although much has been written about how to improve performance appraisal ratings and how to develop better scales for use in evaluating performance, little has been communicated to practicing managers concerning another equally critical area of performance appraisal: the evaluation interview. The interview model presented here is proposed merely as a guide to those managers and supervisors wishing to conduct a performance review that is both accurate and acceptable to all participants concerned. The model does not postulate a "one-best-way" to do so. Rather, it identifies situational characteristics one should consider in deciding how often to conduct a review, what criteria to utilize, and how much participation to allow during the review.

One major conclusion from the model is that the customary once-a-year performance appraisal generally needs to occur more frequently. Further, the model emphasizes a focus on behavior and outcomes rather than on employee traits. Finally, the model favors varying degrees of participation while recognizing that under certain circumstances autocratic approaches to performance appraisal do have their place. But perhaps the most important feature of the model presented here is that it views managers as diagnosticians capable of analyzing these situational variables and modifying their approach accordingly.

1. H. T. Ingle, "Contemporary Issues in Federal Evaluation Policy: New Linkages Between Personnel and Program Assessment Processes," *Public Personnel Management* 11 (Winter 1982): 328.
2. F. J. Thompson, "Performance Appraisal of Public Managers: Inspiration, Consensual Tests and the Margins," *Public Personnel Management* 11 (Winter 1982): 306.
3. P. Allan and S. Rosenberg, "Getting a Managerial Performance Appraisal System Under Way: New York City's Experience," *Public Administration Review* 40 (July–August 1980): 372.
4. N. P. Lovrich, Jr., P. L. Shaffer, R. H. Hopkins, and D. A. Yale, "Do Public Servants Welcome or Fear Merit Evaluation of Their Performance?" *Public Administration Review* 40 (May–June 1980): 214.
5. D. H. Rosenbloom, "Public Sector Performance Appraisal in the Contemporary Legal Environment," *Public Personnel Management* 11 (Winter 1982): 315.
6. B. Giglioni, J. B. Giglioni, and J. A. Bryant, "Performance Appraisal: Here Comes the Judge," *California Management Review* 24 (Winter 1981): 15.
7. H. S. Feild and W. H. Holley, "The Relationship of Performance Appraisal System Characteristics to Verdicts in Selected Employment Discrimination Cases," *Academy of Management Journal* 25 (1982): 398.
8. D. T. Hall and E. E. Lawler, "Unused Potential in Research and Development Organizations," *Research Management* (September 1969): 339.
9. D. R. Ilgen, R. B. Peterson, B. A. Martin, and D. A. Boeschen, "Supervisor and Subordinate Reactions to Performance Appraisal Sessions," *Organizational Behavior and Human Performance* 28 (December 1981): 327.
10. C. H. Fay and G. P. Latham, "Effects of Training and Rating Scales on Rating Errors," *Personnel Psychology* 35 (Spring 1982): 112.
11. J. Nalbandian, "Performance Appraisal: If Only People Were Not Involved," *Public Administration Review* 41 (May–June 1981): 395.
12. K. W. Thomas and W. G. Tymon, Jr., "Necessary Properties of Relevant Research: Lessons from Recent Criticisms of the Organizational Sciences," *Academy of Management Review* 7 (July 1982): 349.
13. M. G. Miner, *Employee Performance Evaluation and Control* (Washington, D.C.: Bureau of National Affairs, 1975), 300.
14. F. J. Landy and J. L. Farr, "Performance Rating," *Psychological Bulletin* 87 (January 1980): 72.
15. Miner, 300.
16. M. Sashkin, "Appraising Appraisal: Ten Lessons from Research for Practice," *Organizational Dynamics* (Winter 1981): 47.
17. M. Beer, "Performance Appraisal: Dilemmas and Possibilities," *Organizational Dynamics* 9 (Winter 1981): 25.
18. D. Cederblom, "The Performance Appraisal Interview: A Review, Implications, and Suggestions," *Acad-*

emy of Management Review 7 (April 1982): 222.

19. Beer, 31.
20. C. D. Fisher and J. Thomas, "The Other Face of Performance Appraisal," *Human Resource Management* 21 (Spring 1982): 25.
21. K. N. Wexley and G. P. Latham, *Developing and Training Human Resources in Organizations* (Glenview, Ill.: Scott, Foresman, 1981), 178.
22. Cederblom, 221.
23. R. W. Woodman and D. C. King, "Organizational Climate: Science or Folklore?" *Academy of Management Review* (October 1978): 817.
24. R. Taguiri and G. H. Litwin, eds., *Organizational Climate: Exploration of a Concept* (Boston: Harvard University, 1968), 27.
25. Feild and Holly, 400.
26. G. B. Brumback and T. S. McFee, "From MBO to MBR," *Public Administration Review* 2 (July–August 1982): 363.
27. D. J. Cherrington, *Personnel Management: The Management of Human Resources* (Dubuque, Iowa: William C. Brown, 1983), 312.
28. M. Keely, "A Contingency Framework for Performance Evaluation," *Academy of Management Review* 3 (July 1978): 434.
29. R. Tannenbaum and W. H. Schmidt, "How to Choose a Leadership Pattern," *Harvard Business Review* (May–June 1973): 180.
30. Cederblom, 220.
31. Wallace and Szilagyi, 1982: 257.
32. W. F. Cascio, "Scientific, Legal, and Operational Imperatives of Workable Performance Appraisal Systems," *Public Personnel Management* (Winter 1982): 373.
33. H. J. Bernardin and R. L. Cardy, "Appraisal Accuracy: The Ability and Motivation to Remember the Past," *Public Personnel Management* 11 (Winter 1982): 356.

34. J. B. Keys and T. R. Miller, "The Japanese Management Theory Jungle, *Academy of Management Review* 9 (April 1984): 349.
35. R. W. Clement, "The Social Science Bias in Management Research: Another View," *Business Horizons* 26 (May–June 1983), 47.
36. Lovrich et al., 220.
37. L. Coch and J. R. P. French, Jr., "Overcoming Resistance to Change," *Human Relations* (August 1948): 512.
38. E. Kay, H. H. Meyer, and J. R. P. French, Jr., "Effects of Threat in a Performance Appraisal Interview," *Journal of Applied Psychology* 50 (October 1965): 311.
39. Cederblom, 225.
40. F. F. Zammuto, M. London, and K. M. Rowland, "Organization and Rater Differences in Performance Appraisals," *Personnel Psychology* 35 (Autumn 1982): 656.
41. W. F. Glueck, *Personnel: A Diagnostic Approach* (Plano, Tex.: Business Publications, 1982), 382.
42. J. R. P. French, Jr., and B. Raven, "The Bases of Social Power," pp. 259–269 in D. Cartwright and A. Zander (eds.), *Group Dynamics* (Evanston, Ill.: Harper and Row, 1968), 262.
43. Ilgen et al., 327.
44. Wexley and Latham, 186.
45. F. E. Fiedler, M. M. Chemers, and L. Mahar, *Improving Leadership Effectiveness: The Leadership Match Concept* (New York: Wiley, 1976).
46. T. R. Mitchell and L. S. Kalb, "Effects of Job Experience or Supervisory Attributions for a Subordinate's Poor Performance," *Journal of Applied Psychology* 67 (April 1982): 188.
47. Cederblom, 226.
48. R. E. Walton and L. A. Schlesinger, "Do Supervisors Thrive in Participative Work Systems?" *Organizational Dynamics* 7 (Winter 1979): 25.

Training the Raters: A Key to Effective Performance Appraisal

David C. Martin and Kathryn M. Bartol

A crucial element in any performance appraisal system is the rater. The rater is the one who makes the actual performance appraisal and conveys that appraisal to the employee. If the rater does not do the job well, the performance appraisal system will not achieve its intended purposes.

Unfortunately, many organizations in both the public and private sectors assume that merely designating an individual as a rater and providing him/her with some paper instructions is sufficient to ensure effective rater participation. Yet there is ample evidence that raters must be trained to successfully carry out their roles in a performance appraisal system.[1]

Although various writers have mentioned specific areas where training is needed, the major elements which should comprise rater training are typically ignored. The purpose of this article is to outline the major areas which should be included in an effective rater training program. The training areas are listed in Table 1 and will be discussed in turn. The training could be conducted as an intensive two-day program or could be spread out over several days, with selected segments being presented each day. Recommended lengths for each training segment for an initial rater training program are included in Table 1.

Performance appraisal as a management tool

The primary objective of performance appraisal is the improvement of organizational productivity. In this role, performance appraisal is a powerful managerial tool. However, appropriate training is necessary to help managers appreciate the value of performance ap-

Reprinted with permission of the International Personnel Management Association from the Summer 1986 issue of *Public Personnel Management*.

Table 1. Major elements of initial rater training program.

Element	Typical time (in hours)
Performance appraisal as a management tool	1
Organization's performance appraisal system	2
Setting standards	2
Rater as a leader and a coach	1
Typical rating errors and how to avoid them	5
What the rater can expect from the system	1
Performance appraisal interview	3
Total	15

praisal in assisting them to realize their organizational objectives. Such training should be aimed at a conceptual understanding of performance appraisal as a management system through which the behaviors required by the organization are transmitted, reinforced, and rewarded. The performance appraisal system provides a means through which criteria governing the performance for each member of the organization are established. It also constitutes the vehicle through which the organization's rating as to how well the individual meets the criteria is conveyed and appropriate rewards are determined. Performance appraisal allows the organization to place special emphasis on specific areas which it deems particularly important. For example, if an organization believes that its managers should be supporting the organizational affirmative action program, that issue can be addressed as part of the performance appraisal process. Helping raters to understand the usefulness of performance appraisal as a management tool enhances their participation in making the system a success.

The organization's performance appraisal system

Since performance appraisal systems should be tailored to the needs of the particular organization, system parameters can vary greatly from one organization to another. As a result, it is important that raters be trained to understand the specific characteristics of the performance appraisal system of their own organization.

For example, performance appraisal results can be used for numerous purposes, depending on choices made by the organization. The purposes include selection, promotion, compensation, training and development, career counseling, motivation, feedback, human resource planning, determination of layoffs and terminations, and validations of studies. It is important that raters be aware of the intended purposes of their ratings. A study by Zedeck and Cascio indicates that raters vary their ratings depending on their understanding of uses which will be made of the ratings.[2] Without appropriate training, such tendencies can become major contaminants in the system.

The type of rating technique used (e.g., management by objectives, behaviorally anchored rating scales, or graphic rating scales) also must be carefully explained, with particular emphasis on the attendant strengths, weaknesses, and pitfalls.[3] Raters must have a thorough understanding of the meaning of the various dimensions to be rated, the weights placed on them, objectives to be set, etc., in order to utilize a particular technique properly.

Raters also need to be well versed in the logistical aspects of the system, such as when ratings are to be conducted, where the various forms are to be sent, and when. If the system is to have reviewers of the ratings, the role of the reviewers in the process must be understood by all parties so that the reviewer role is one which supports the process rather than one which breeds misunderstanding. In addition, raters should be well informed regarding the employee appeal process in order to be able to adequately explain the process, when necessary, to those individuals whom they will subsequently appraise.

Setting standards

A main function of the rater in performance appraisal is to facilitate the setting of performance standards.[4] Raters should be trained to set standards with or without assistance from the employee being rated. One means of setting standards is through goal setting—a performance appraisal system used extensively in both the public and private sectors. Since the passage of the Civil Service Reform Act of 1978, for example, a performance appraisal system based on goal setting has been used in the federal government. In the case of goal setting, research indicates that participation by employees in setting goals may be beneficial because the subordinate, rather than the superior, has the information necessary to establish goals and their supporting action plans.[5] In many organizations where employees participate in the goal setting process, they develop the goals and then bring them to the manager for approval. However, the rater must ensure that the goals are measurable, realistic and challenging in order for the system to work properly.[6] Without appropriate training, raters are rarely equipped to guide the goal setting process adequately.

With other types of systems, such as behaviorally anchored rating scales (BARS), the rater must also be able to articulate clearly the standards upon which the ratee will be evaluated. Unless the rater has a good understanding of the BARS to be used, for example, the rater may faslely convey to the ratee that he/she will be rated on the specific anchors, rather than explaining that the anchors will be used as a basis for observations about job related behaviors.[7] Thus it is quite easy for both the rater and the ratee to become confused about just how the rating process works, causing it to fail to achieve its intended purposes.

In addition to establishing effective performance standards, raters must make certain that resources, such as time, people, and raw materials, are available to those employees who require them to accomplish their assigned tasks properly. The timing of these resources is normally critical to the completion of such tasks. Therefore, raters should be trained to discuss resources requirements in conjunction with standard setting.

Typical rating errors and how to avoid them

Although some performance appraisal methods are better than others, none is immune to a variety of common rating errors.[8] Through training it is possible at least to eliminate many of these errors and to improve the accuracy of performance appraisals. The typical rating errors are explained below.

Perhaps the most researched rating errors are those of halo and leniency/stringency. The halo effect is the rating of an employee excellent in one quality, which in turn influences the rater to give that employee a similar rating on other qualities.[9] Leniency/stringency—or severity, as it is sometimes called—is the general tendency to assign extreme ratings.[10] Thus, if the rater is asked to rate a number of individuals on a series of items from poor to excellent, the rater tends to rate most items either on the poor or the excellent end of the scales, depending on the individual being rated.

The contrast effect error is the tendency for the rater to evaluate an employee in relation to other employees rather than on the requirements of the job.[11] Under certain conditions, this tendency can lead to serious errors. For example, if the other workers are poor performers, an average worker may receive an excellent rating.

The similar-to-me effect is the tendency to rate an individual according to how the rater views the rated employee in relation to him/herself.[12] The closer the rated individual is to how the rater views him/herself, the higher the rating the individual tends to subsequently receive.

The error of central tendency is the rating of all individuals in the middle of the scale.[13] It is the "safe" rating, since no one receives particularly good or particularly poor ratings. The normal impact of this type of error is that it adversely affects particularly good performers while being overly generous with poor performers who would ordinarily be rated on the low extreme of the scale.

The first impression error is the result of a manager or supervisor making an initial evaluation of an individual which then overshadows what the individual does during the rating period.[14] If the first impression is positive, the supervisor or manager will recognize the positive contributions, but overlook or ignore the less than positive actions by the individual being rated.

The recency effect error is the weighting of those activities which have been completed near the time of the formal appraisal more heavily than those which were completed early in the rating period.[15] This tendency can lead to unfair results, particularly when there are a number of negative occurrences related to performance just before the performance appraisal is scheduled to be done.

Numerous other errors have also been reported in conjunction with performance appraisals, including loss of detail through simplification, overdependence on a single source, categorization error (forcing observations into categories instead of remembering the differences between ideas, behaviors, and people), contextual errors (letting the situation or setting influence observations), and prejudice and stereotyping.[16]

A number of studies indicate that through training it is possible to reduce major rating errors on performance appraisals. One general approach that has been successful in such training is the use of rating simulations, such as video tapes and role plays. Trainees prepare ratings which then are compared to appropriate solutions in order to identify rating errors and learn to correct them.[17]

Many rating errors can be traced to the cognitive limitations of the raters, such as memory capacities and the ability to gather adequate information to make performance judgments.[18] As a result, an effective training program should emphasize techniques for gathering appropriate information to conduct a performance appraisal. One approach which has proved to be effective is to train raters to keep a diary of particularly good behaviors and particularly poor behaviors of employees (i.e., critical incidents) which are then useful in providing a more adequate sampling of job behaviors for performance rating purposes.[19] Research by Spool demonstrates that training programs for observers of behavior normally consist of some mix of lecture, demonstration, practice, and feedback (usually through a discussion).[20]

The time required to train raters to preclude or eliminate rating errors is another issue to be recognized when preparing a rater training program. Although in some studies the training was minimal (e.g., a few minutes), such training could require about one and a half to two hours per error for a particularly complex type of error such as the contrast effect effort. Thus the training of raters to preclude potential and existing errors will require a substantial amount of time. Yet the resultant quality of appraisals should more than compensate for the training time expended. One workable strategy is to provide training on several of the major errors in an initial training program such as is outlined in Table 1 and then reinforce and expand the training through feedback systems and later refresher training.

What the rater can expect from the system

Raters should be able to expect certain types of feedback from a performance appraisal system, yet raters do not habitually receive such feedback. A survey by the Conference Board of 293 major industrial firms revealed that three-fourths of the firms indicated that performance appraisals were reviewed by the rater's immediate supervisor.[21] However, not a single firm provided ongoing systems guidance to raters concerning rating errors and how to correct them.

As part of the performance appraisal system, raters should receive feedback concerning the manner in which they perform their performance appraisal role. Appraisals should be monitored for such issues as timeliness of submission, completeness of ratings, evidence of rating errors, quality of ratings, and consistency of ratings. Feedback should be specific, addressing issues which raters can be expected to correct or continue. Longitudinal date should be maintained for each rater for comparison with prior years, to enable the system to pinpoint rating errors across a number of performance appraisals by the same rater. This would help to reinforce the effects of the rater training by providing data which raters can use to monitor their rating behaviors.

Raters should also be able to expect a high relationship between the ratings they give and the rewards available to their employees. If an employee receives a high rating, the employee should be rewarded in some manner, e.g., pay raise, promotion, training, individual recognition, and assignments. Performance appraisals work most effectively as motivational tools when individuals in the organization perceive a clear link between individual performance and organizational rewards.

The rater as a leader and a coach

Raters normally have a designated function as leader and coach of those they appraise. In this capacity, raters set an example by their interest in setting reasonable but challenging work standards. However, raters also must be sensitive to the development needs of the individuals being rated.

As a coach, the rater has the responsibility to ensure that employees are trained to accomplish assigned work. A part of this responsibility includes observing the manner in which the employee performs the job. The rater must furnish the necessary help, guidance, and assistance required not only to ensure immediate job success, but also to develop the employee to his/her greatest potential.

Many performance appraisal systems include a provision which recognizes the professional development of subordinates.

Performance feedback is particularly important to both the rater and the employee being appraised.[22] It is the medium by which the employee learns of recognized accomplishments or failures to meet organizational goals. It is an opportunity for raters to coach employees by providing reinforcement for tasks well done and assistance in those areas where improvements are required. The best results are obtained when feedback is continuous, consistent, conducted on an informal basis, and is furnished immediately when an employee completes or fails to complete a task.

Fulfilling the coach role involves an understanding of such factors as how people learn, the need to provide positive reinforcement, the need to maintain two-way communications, and the requirement to provide adequate resources to do the job. Because the role of coach is a continuous process which is fundamental to the success of a performance appraisal system, it is vital to provide training to raters. Such training should take the form of case studies, role plays, behavioral modeling, and discussions aimed at increasing the coaching skills of raters.

The performance appraisal interview

The annual performance appraisal interview should be a discussion which centers on reviewing the documentation of the work performed during the rating period and, even more importantly, on mutually setting goals for the next period. Three common approaches to the performance appraisal interview have been noted by Maier.[23] These are: tell and sell, tell and listen, and problem solving. The tell and sell approach includes informing employees how well they are doing and may include subsequently setting goals for improvement for them. The tell and listen approach places the rater in the role of the listener after having informed the employee of his/her performance. Frequently no goals are set and the rater concentrates on listening once the initial evaluation has been given. In the problem solving approach, rater and ratee mutually discuss both strong and weak areas. Then, while discussing how the weaker areas can be improved, they jointly set goals. The rater concentrates on removing obstacles to the performance of the employee and furnishing assistance where possible. This latter method, as noted by Maier, has proven to be generally the most effective approach.

In support of Maier's view, research by Burke, Weitzel, and Weir has highlighted several characteristics of effective performance appraisal interviews.[24] These are:

1. High levels of ratee participation in the performance appraisal process lead to greater ratee satisfaction with the appraisal process and the rater.

2. Ratees are more satisfied with the performance appraisal interview when the rater adapts a helpful and constructive attitude.
3. Mutual setting of specific goals to be achieved by the ratee leads to twice as much improvement in subsequent performance as does either a discussion of general goals or criticism.
4. Solution of problems which may be interfering with the ratee's work leads to direct performance improvements.
5. The amount of criticism given by the rater is related to the degree of defensive reaction by the ratee. In fact, little or no performance improvement can be expected in areas that are heavily criticized.

The success of the appraisal interview, then, depends largely on the skills of the rater. As a result, rater training on effectively carrying out an appraisal interview is a vital link in an effective performance appraisal system. Through the use of role plays, explanations, video tapes, and behavioral modeling, it is possible to train raters to conduct interviews that lead to fewer defensive reactions from ratees and more productive results in terms of future performance.[25] Bernardin and Buckley argue that one reason why supervisors are overly lenient in performance appraisal ratings is that they feel ill equipped to cope with negative reactions from subordinates regarding appraisals.[26] Training aimed at increasing appraisal interview skills, and particularly at handling below-standard performers, can help raters gain confidence in their abilities to successfully deal with a variety of appraisal situations.

Need for refresher training

Like any working device, the performance appraisal system must be monitored to ensure that it is meeting its intended goals. The raters must play a major role in ensuring that the system continues to function as intended. In order for the raters to execute properly their role over a period of time, they must receive refresher training. Research by Ivancevich found that raters who participated in an intensive training program made fewer psychometric errors in ratings than those who were not trained.[27] However, the training effects began to dissipate after 6 to 12 months, indicating the need to provide reinforcement and refresher training. In addition, many of the behaviors necessary to function as an effective rater will take time to develop, even though an initial training program is an important beginning. Therefore, as a minimum, there should be short, substantive performance appraisal training sessions conducted for raters on an annual basis. This training could be done in conjunction with other continuing management development training programs and should both reinforce and build on previous training. Only through this continuous process can the performance appraisal system have the desired effect on productivity.

Conclusion

Since the rater is the main interface between the performance appraisal system and the ratee, behaviors of the rater will have a strong bearing on the ratee's reaction to the system and his/her subsequent performance. As a result, it is vitally important that raters be trained to fulfill their appraisal function adequately. This article outlines the major elements which should comprise rater training. First, raters need to acquire a thorough understanding of the usefulness of performance appraisal as a management tool. Second, training is necessary regarding the specific characteristics of the performance appraisal system used in the organization, including the appeals process. Third, raters must to be able to set meaningful performance standards, the basis for performance maintenance and improvement. Fourth, raters need to learn how to avoid common psychometric errors and to gather appropriate information on which to base their performance appraisals. Fifth, raters should know what to expect from the system in terms of feedback, including rewards to ratees. Sixth, training is necessary in order to assist raters in their roles as leaders and coaches within the performance appraisal framework. Seventh, conducting effective performance appraisal interviews requires skill levels which most raters will find difficult to acquire without training. Finally, the necessity for refresher training for raters should be recognized and programmed as part of the training process. Well trained raters add immeasurably to the success of the performance appraisal process and to subsequent organizational productivity.

1. For example, W. H. Cooper, "Ubiquitous Halo," *Psychological Bulletin* 90 (1981):218-44; and G. P. Latham and K. N. Wexley, *Increasing Productivity Through Performance Appraisal* (Reading, Mass.: Addison-Wesley Publishing Co., Inc., 1981).

2. S. Zedeck and W. F. Cascio, "Performance Appraisal Decisions as a Function of Rater Training and Purpose of the Appraisal," *Journal of Applied Psychology* 67 (1982): 752-58.

3. A. S. DeNisi, T. P. Cafferty, and B. M. Meglino, "A Cognitive View of the Performance Appraisal Process: A Model and Research Propositions," *Organizational Behavior and Human Performance* 33 (1984): 360-96.

4. W. C. Borman, "Forman and Training Effects on Rating Accuracy and Rater Errors," *Journal of Applied Psychology* 64 (1979):410-21.

5. S. J. Carroll and C. E. Schneier, *Performance Appraisal and Review Systems* (Glenview, Ill.: Scott, Foresman and Company, 1982).

6. G. P. Latham and E. A. Locke, *Goal Setting: A Motivational Technique That Works* (Englewood Cliffs, N.J.: Prentice-Hall, 1984).

7. H. J. Bernardin and P. C. Smith, "A Clarification of Some Issues Regarding the Development and Use of Behaviorally Anchored Rating

Scales," *Journal of Applied Psychology* 66 (1981):458–63.

8. Ibid.

9. R. I. Henderson, *Performance Appraisal* (Reston, Va.: Reston Publishing Co., Inc., 1984).

10. H. J. Bernardin and R. W. Beatty, *Performance Appraisal: Assessing Human Behavior at Work* (Boston, Mass.: Kent Publishing Company, 1984).

11. K. N. Wexley, R. E. Sanders, and G. A. Yukl, "Training Interviewers to Eliminate Contrast Effects in Employment Interviews," *Journal of Applied Psychology* 57 (1973): 233–36.

12. Latham and Wexley, 1981.

13. Carroll and Schneier, 1982.

14. Bernardin and Beatty, 1984.

15. Ibid.

16. G. C. Thornton, III, and S. Zorich, "Training to Improve Observer Accuracy," *Journal of Applied Psychology* 65 (1980):351–59.

17. H. J. Bernardin, "Effects of Rater Training on Leniency and Halo Errors in Student Ratings of Instructors," *Journal of Applied Psychology* 63 (1973):301–308; H. J. Bernardin and C. S. Walter, "Effects of Rater Training and Diary-Keeping on Psychometric Error in Ratings," *Journal of Applied Psychology* 60 (1975):556–60; W. C. Borman, "Effects of Instruction to Avoid Halo Error on Reliability and Validity of Performance Evaluation Ratings," *Journal of Applied Psychology* 60 (1975):556–60; W. C. Borman, "Forman and Training Effects on Rating Accuracy and Rater Errors,"

Journal of Applied Psychology 64 (1979):410–21; J. M. Ivancevich, "Longitudinal Study of the Effects of Rater Training on Psychometric Error in Ratings," *Journal of Applied Psychology* 64 (1979):502–09; D. L. Warmcke and R. S. Billings, "Comparison of Training Methods for Improving the Psychometric Quality of Experimental and Administrative Performance Ratings," *Journal of Applied Psychology* 64 (1979): 123–31.

18. Ilgen and Feldman, 1983.

19. H. J. Bernardin and M. R. Buckley, "Strategies in Rater Training," *Academy of Management Review* 6 (1981):205–12.

20. M. D. Spool, "Training Programs for Observers of Behavior: A Review," *Personnel Psychology* 31 (1978): 853–88.

21. R. I. Lazer and W. S. Wisktrom, *Appraising Managerial Performance: Current Practices and Future Directions* (New York: Conference Board, 1977).

22. Latham and Wexley, 1981.

23. N. R. F. Maier, *The Appraisal Interview: Three Basic Approaches* (La Jolla, Calif.: University Associates, 1976).

24. R. J. Burke, R. J. Weitzel, and T. Weir, "Characteristics of Effective Employee Performance Review and Development Interviews: Replication and Extention," *Personnel Psychology* 31 (1978):903–19.

25. Spool, 1978.

26. Bernardin and Buckley, 1981.

27. Ivancevich, 1979.

Performance Appraisal: Improving the Rater's Effectiveness

David C. Martin

In their search for methods of increasing employee productivity, many organizations have adopted performance appraisal systems. Essentially, these systems are based on a four-step process in which performance goals are established, work standards are communicated, job performance is monitored, and feedback on accomplishments and areas that need improvement is given. Successful completion of each step depends on honest, clear, easily understood communications between supervisor and rated employee.

All too frequently, however, communications between rater and rated employee are garbled or less than frank. In some cases, communication may be virtually nonexistent. As a result, an organization may experience a serious loss of productivity. Employees who receive misleading information about their job performance may face dire consequences. Raters, too, may suffer directly when their units do not perform as required. A court case, *Chamberlain* v. *Bissell Inc.*, illustrates some additional consequences that may occur when raters fail to properly conduct performance reviews.

Guilty of negligence

During his annual performance review, John Chamberlain, a manager of manufacturing engineering at Bissell Inc., was informed that he would not receive a wage increase that year because essential objectives for his department had not been achieved. Until then, Chamberlain had regularly received wage increases. In explaining the reason for denying a wage increase, the rater reminded Chamberlain that he had failed to respond to repeated requests for creating a better incentive system, that morale in his department was low, that he was difficult to work with, and that he had to be pressured to complete projects. The rater concluded the performance review by saying, "You have a lot of talent. We haven't decided what to do with you."

Chamberlain understood that the rater was dissatisfied with some parts of his performance, but he believed that the primary reason for the rater's dissatisfaction could be attributed to the fact that his department was understaffed. Furthermore, during the review, the rater never indicated that Chamberlain had been or might soon be considered for dismissal. Yet just a little more than two months later, Chamberlain, an employee of 23 years, was fired.

The reasons cited for Chamberlain's release were his poor attitude, lack of cooperation, lack of leadership, failure to take over parts of a job that had been combined with his, and failure to develop a new incentive system. Each of these issues had been discussed with him previously, some on several occasions. However, the possibility or probability of being fired had never been discussed with Chamberlain prior to his dismissal.

The court indicated that a reasonable person (in this case the rater) under the circumstances would have told Chamberlain that discharge was being considered—or at least was possible. Since the rater had failed to give Chamberlain this warning, the court concluded that the rater had been negligent. The court considered the following points in reaching this conclusion:

1. The rater knew, or should have known, that Chamberlain would expect to be given notice of an impending discharge, at least if the discharge was being considered at the time of his annual performance review.
2. The rater knew, or should have known, that Chamberlain's 22 years of adequate service tended to create a heightened sense of job security on his part—an impression that the rater knew to be unjustified.
3. The rater knew, or should have known, that Chamberlain's previous evaluations had been relatively adequate, if not good; that Chamberlain had had no previous reason to fear for his job; and that Chamberlain's decline in performance was directly related to his failure to be named a vice-president.
4. The rater's failure to specifically inform Chamberlain of the possibility of discharge served no identifiable employer interest that would justify the risk it imposed on Chamberlain.

In summing up the case, the court indicated that the rater was in a position to eliminate all doubt concerning Chamberlain's status and, further, to provide Chamberlain with the greatest possible incentive to reform his conduct and improve his performance. Since the rater had no reason not to take the necessary step of informing Chamberlain, the rater's failure to do so could be properly labeled as negligent.

Moreover, the court argued that the company had a duty of reasonable care. By failing to inform Chamberlain about possible dismissal, the company increased the risk that he would ultimately be discharged. Failure to notify Chamberlain that he may or could be discharged if there was not a dramatic change in his performance was not justified by any counterbalancing benefit or interest. Therefore, Bissell Inc. did not live up to (breached) its duty of ordinary care.

Under Michigan law (where this case was argued), the duty of ordinary care arises from performance of a contractual obligation. In this instance, there was no contract (that is, a specific written procedure indicating that raters must inform rated employees that they must improve their performance or be discharged). Consequently, failure to warn Chamberlain that he might be discharged was regarded as negligent performance of the employer's obligation and was classified as a tort rather than a breach of contract.

The court also recognized that Chamberlain had been largely responsible for his discharge, citing his poor attitude, conduct, and job performance that had been discussed with him on many occasions as well as his failure to be more active in defining his status. As a result, the court concluded that Chamberlain was 83% responsible for bringing about his own discharge, and Bissell Inc. was responsible for the remaining 17%. The pecuniary award to Chamberlain that accompanied this judgment was 17% of $360,906, or $61,354.

More substance needed

Chamberlain v. *Bissell Inc.* clearly illustrates the human problems and loss of productivity associated with the failure to conduct adequate performance reviews. It also highlights the growing legal problems for organizations in which managers do not appraise employees' performance carefully and effectively. To avoid these problems, performance reviews must accurately reflect an employee's performance on the job and clearly identify any areas that need improvement as well as the consequences of failing to meet stated objectives.

The key to more substantive performance reviews is preparation by both the rater and the rated employee. The rater should review the rated employee's job functions, work standards, achievements, qualifications for higher-level jobs in the organization, and areas in which formal or informal training would enhance the individual's potential and career.

Therefore, the rater needs to keep a journal on the rated employee's accomplishments during the period to be reviewed. Alternately, the rated employee can keep a journal to which both parties refer during the performance appraisal. Recording accomplishments when they happen greatly increases the accuracy of the evaluation and reduces the possibility of rating employees on the basis of their most recent accomplishments.

Employees, too, should prepare for performance reviews. They should compare job performance with previously established standards, assess career objectives both within the organization and their career field, and draft work goals for the forthcoming period. If performance reviews are done quarterly or semiannually, goals for the remainder of the rating period should be emphasized, with some discussion of the goals for the following rating period.

The rater's three roles

In conducting an effective performance review, raters must play three somewhat conflicting roles: coach, leader and allocator of resources, and judge. They must objectively evaluate an employee's job performance from each of these perspectives.

As a coach, the rater is responsible for developing employees to their fullest potential. To fulfill this responsibility, the rater may recommend training, job rotation, or a special assignment. As a leader and allocator of resources, the rater is responsible for ensuring that resources required to accomplish assigned goals are made available to the rated employee when needed. Otherwise, the goal must be modified to compensate for the lack of resources. As a judge, the rater must evaluate the achievements of the rated employee while also considering the degree of difficulty of the assignment and the resources furnished to the employee to accomplish the assignment.

During a performance review, these three roles may become difficult to segregate. For example, if as a judge the rater believes an employee's job performance to be below par, the rater must assume the role of leader and allocator of resources to consider whether the proper job assignment and level of accomplishment were assigned originally. Also in this role, the rater must review the availability of resources in terms of both quantity and timeliness to ensure that the rated employee had what was required to meet the original expected level of achievement. Finally, as a coach, the rater must evaluate each accomplishment or lack of accomplishment. The employee's strengths must be properly nurtured, while the employee's weaknesses must be given the attention needed to make them strengths.

The method of conducting a performance review may help the rater emphasize one or more of these roles. Whatever method is selected, it should enable employees to increase productivity and subsequently their value to the organization.

Choosing an appropriate method of review

Because work environments and relationships between supervisor and employee differ in many respects, the method used for performance reviews may also vary. Norman Maier, former professor of psychology, has suggested the following three methods of conducting performance reviews: the tell-and-sell method, the tell-and-listen method, and the problem-solving method.

Tell-and-sell method   With this type of performance review, the rater tells the rated employee how well he or she is doing and attempts to persuade (sell) the employee to set goals for improvement. This method is likely to be most effective when an authoritarian leadership style is practiced. Interpersonal communications flow downward, from supervisor (rater) to the lower-level rated employee, with the rater dominating the conversation. As a result, the tell-and-sell method of performance review requires much less time to complete than the other methods.

However, this type of review can adversely affect the relationship between supervisor and employee. Employees' job performance may deteriorate when they believe that their interests and their supervisor's interests conflict. The day-to-day relationship between the two parties may become strained, causing a less than desirable work relationship in the future.

Further, the dynamics of having the supervisor play the dominant role during performance reviews may cause some employees to become totally acquiescent, thus prohibiting very valuable feedback from being given to the rater. Alternately, some employees may become contentious, arguing constantly with their supervisor as a means of displaying self-identify. Either reaction is disruptive to a smooth work relationship.

Thus the tell-and-sell method appears to be best suited to situations in which a supervisor is strong-minded and requires little feedback from employees. It is also appropriate when a rater wants to emphasize the role of judge rather than the roles of coach and leader.

Tell-and-listen method   This type of performance review encourages greater interaction between rater and rated employee. The rater informs the rated employee how well assigned duties have been performed and points out the employee's strengths as well as areas that need improvement. The rater then listens closely to the employee's response. From this response, the rater determines the rated employee's attitudes and feelings, which are then discussed. The goal of this discussion is to maximize the employee's satisfaction with the job.

This type of performance review may be effective in situations in which work relationships are highly collegial in nature (such as in voluntary organizations) and are based on an overriding need for employees to derive a high degree of satisfaction from their jobs and motivation from the review process. Using the tell-and-listen method, the rater acts primarily as a judge and to a lesser extent as a coach and allocator of resources.

Problem-solving method   The most frequently recommended and used type of performance review, the problem-solving method emphasizes the removal of obstacles to good performance. These obstacles may be work procedures or practices, lack of resources, lack of certain skills, or misunderstandings about the requirements of the job. Setting goals for the subsequent rating period is a major aspect of this type of performance review, whereas it is not normally a part of the tell-and-sell or the tell-and-listen methods.

The problem-solving method is therefore based on open, clear, two-way communications between rater and rated employee. Both must fully participate in reviewing accomplishments, recognizing areas in which additional emphasis is needed, and determining how improvements will be made. The rater must be prepared to discuss the employee's work performance as well as techniques for assisting the employee. The rated employee must be prepared to discuss his or her accomplishments, current and future resource requirements, short-term and long-term career objectives, and goals for the forthcoming rating period.

The problem-solving method can be used in most situations. Because it is relatively nonthreatening and therefore reduces any hostility that employees may feel during performance reviews, raters who understand this method will normally use it. With the problem-solving method, the rater acts in all three roles—judge, leader, and coach—with particular emphasis on the roles of leader and coach.

Some lessons learned

Several important lessons can be learned from *Chamberlain* v. *Bissell Inc.* By adapting the following suggestions, organizations can help their employees make the performance appraisal process more effective:

First, an organization should establish performance review procedures that produce stimulating, frank, and motivating discussions between rater and rated employee. These vital reviews must be scheduled and be an integral part of the overall performance appraisal process. Organizations should specify the timing of performance reviews (for example, monthly, quarterly, semiannually, or annually) as well as the purpose and issues to be included. They also should have a procedure for ensuring that reviews are completed in accordance with the schedule.

It should be noted that Bissell Inc. had a requirement for annual performance reviews for all employees. The court determined that the performance reviews were intended, in part, to benefit Bissell's employees by informing them of their supervisor's perceptions of their performance. However, the company's policy did not indicate that future goals and the career development of employees were required to be discussed during performance reviews. This type of requirement might have forced a discussion of Chamberlain's future with the organization, thereby preventing costly litigation.

Second, since much of the success of performance reviews depends on the interpersonal skills of the rater, raters should be trained to properly execute this vital management function. Role-playing exercises, explanations, videotapes, and behavior modeling can be used to train raters to conduct interviews that lead to fewer defensive reactions on the part of rated employees and more productive results in terms of future job performance. Some techniques for more effective performance reviews are listed in Exhibit 1.

Third, organizations need a clear, easily understood policy on action to be taken when an employee's job performance is unacceptable. Bissell Inc. had a policy on discharging salaried employees that specifically addressed incompetence, insubordination, misconduct, and attendance as reasons for dismissal. However, the policy did not require notice to be given, either explicitly or implicitly, to the employee prior to dismissal. Further, it did not specify that employees should be given an opportunity to improve their performance prior to discharge. This latter point became one of the central issues in *Chamberlain* v. *Bissell Inc.*

The value of allowing employees to rectify poor performance was recognized on a large scale in 1978 when, as part of establishing new performance appraisal systems, most federal agencies were ordered to include in their performance appraisal systems a provision for "assisting employees in improving unacceptable performance" and for "reassigning, reducing in grade, or removing employees who continue to have unacceptable performance, but only after an opportunity to demonstrate acceptable performance" (Public Law 95-454). This kind of provision would probably benefit most organizations. Of even greater benefit would be the recognition by raters that an employee's future with the organization should be discussed during performance appraisals.

Exhibit 1. Techniques for more effective performance reviews.

Raters should be trained to conduct a performance review. This training should address preparation for the review, purpose of the review, method to be used, techniques for recognizing and removing obstacles to performance, techniques for setting performance goals, and career-development counseling for rated employees.

Performance reviews should be conducted in accordance with an organizational schedule (for example, quarterly, semiannually, or annually).

Employees should be notified in advance and asked to prepare themselves to discuss their job performance, future goals, and career aspirations.

Raters should be prepared to discuss the rated employee's job performance, impediments to good job performance, training that could benefit the employee, and future goals for the employee.

At the conclusion of the performance review, the rater and the rated employee should have a clear understanding of the employee's job performance during the previous rating period, goals for the future, and areas in which the employee needs and will receive career assistance.

Fourth, organizations should have a system for evaluating the manner in which raters execute the performance-appraisal process. Employee-attitude surveys are one means by which raters and organizations can get valuable feedback on the performance appraisal process. In addition, raters who conduct effective performance reviews should be recognized for this achievement when their performance is appraised.

In summary, a well-conducted performance review can lead to a better understanding of the rated employee's accomplishments, future goals, and career-development requirements. Similarly, effective communications between rater and rated employee can improve the employee's job satisfaction and productivity and reduce voluntary turnover.

Practical Management Series

**Performance Evaluation:
An Essential Management Tool**

Text type
Century Expanded

Composition
Unicorn Graphics
Washington, D.C.

Printing and binding
R. R. Donnelley & Sons Company
Harrisonburg, Virginia

Cover design
Rebecca Geanaros